Chuck & Michele

Rochelle & Chuckie
Michele & Chuck

Chuckie
(Chooky)

Ricky

One Year One Month and One day
(Italian Twins)

Me with my Godfather Big Al
and Tony Brush from Cleveland's Little Italy in Murray Hill

Mom (2004) giving out pretzels
like she used to at Neddie's
beverage back in the 50's.

Chuck and his dad at their East Cleveland home (1968)

A MAN OF HIS WORD

My Walk, My Witness

by
Chuck Rambaldo

One man's journey that achieved the American Dream and eventually led to despair, depression, and deliverance.

authorHOUSE®

AuthorHouse™
1663 Liberty Drive
Bloomington, IN 47403
www.authorhouse.com
Phone: 1-800-839-8640

First published by AuthorHouse 11/23/2009

ISBN: 978-1-4389-8800-9 (sc)

Library of Congress Control Number: 2009905278

Printed in the United States of America
Bloomington, Indiana

This book is printed on acid-free paper.

DEDICATION

To my deceased relatives, especially my dad, Frank, and my father-in-law, Dave Morad, Sr., and my son-in-law, Mat Bailey; my Grandma Mary and Grandma Lucy, and my Uncle Arnold and my Uncle John Paschull, and my Aunt Cora Gianatonio and Aunt Eve Morad.

ACKNOWLEDGMENTS

I wish to thank all of our families and friends who have shared my life's memories. They have helped me not only to shape this book but to shape my life:

My wife, Michele, who has been with me through thick and thin. When I nicknamed her "Mush" years ago, it was for the way she constantly displayed love and caring for all those with whom she came in contact. Now, thirty-six years later, Michele has turned that "Mush" in my life into a loving wife, mother, grandmother, and my best friend;

Our children, Rochelle and Chuckie; my mother, Mary Ann (Neddie); my brother Rick; my brothers-in-law, David and Ricky; Aunt Cora and all my aunts, uncles and cousins, especially Joe Comai;

Jerry and Grace Wrobel and their prayer group; Marcia Ostrowski; JoAnn Odell; the families of Accurate Die Casting; Dave and Alice Morad; my editor, Patricia Mote; my photo editor, Gina Marie Criscione; Dion DiMucci; the late Tim Russert; Ernie Sobieski; Terry Drake; Richard Richards and Mike Young.

A person I am indebted to for helping me get started on this book is Jerry Lynn Hartley. She said, "Let it be known that this story is being told in memorable increments. It is a story that will touch on some childhood memories, some courtship memories, but mostly the memories and formation of an adult facing life's dilemmas and overcoming obstacles to achieve happiness and inner peace. It is the sole purpose of this manuscript to give credit where credit is due and to gift the reader with proof that the truth will set a man free."

C. R.

INTRODUCTION

My people are destroyed for lack of knowledge. The words of God were written for our instruction, to teach and train us. Written in the pages of the Bible are truths of life, health, and peace. If we fail, through these truths we can stand again. Through embracing these truths, we are healed if sickness comes. Hosea 4: 6.

Not by might nor by power, but by Spirit says the Lord Almighty. We have already claimed victory in the Lord. Zechariah 4: 6.

Almost every one of us has viewed that famous scene from the movie *The Blues Brothers* where John Belushi is asked by the Godfather of Soul, James Brown, "Do you see the light?" When there is a look of confusion on his face, Brown repeats his question more emphatically. "DO YOU SEE THE LIGHT?"

Instantly Belushi shouts back, "I do. I do see the light."

As the old saying goes, it only happens in the movies. Every one of us has been down due to life's quick twists and turns. It seems that when we are the one affected—we want a quick fix. Unlike Belushi's experience, most of us have to wait longer than we expect. I had to learn that we win the battles in this world by not being of the world but by simply surrendering.

In my case, I had to learn that when I was asked the question, "Do you see the light?" I answered Yes, yet I knew not of what I spoke. Jesus is the Way, the Truth, and the Light. It is my intent to share my life's experiences thus far with the hope that they might plant a seed or be a witness to those who are traveling down life's journey and find themselves wading, floating, or drowning in the deep waters or trials.

There is hope—hope in our Savior, Jesus Christ. He is truly the only Man of His Word into whom we should tap.

My education in business taught me that preparation is ninety percent of the battle. When it came to the business world, I executed ten percent above normal. Basically, I was prepared. But I had to find out the hard way that when it came to the spiritual warfare I would face, I was only ten percent prepared when I needed to be able to execute ninety percent.

There is a special place in my heart for all of the men who pretend to belong to a group that proudly states, "I've got it all together because I'm a member of the three-piece men-of-steel suits club!" We were educated and trained that we proud men have to win! Win at any cost. I still have a Vince Lombardi plaque, which used to hang in my corporate office, entitled What It Takes to Be No. 1: There's no room for second place. There is only one place in my game and that is first place. Winning is not a sometime thing; it's an all-time thing.

If you have chosen to be of this world, that's exactly what you are judged by: your title, your home, your appearance, your car, and your salary. Initially, a man cannot be blamed for striving to achieve all of these accomplishments. After all, those are what we are taught are true symbols of worldly success. Sooner or later, we all run out of the energy required to keep all of this stuff up. If you find yourself running on empty, what follows in this book may help to put a tiger back in your tank.

I failed miserably in the battle of something I knew little of, the battle of the mind. The spiritual realm we face daily is one that few of us are totally prepared to face. When we are going through life's trials, we have to remember that others (our family, our spouses, our children, our parents, our brothers, our sisters, our business associates and our friends) are watching how we react and handle them. DON'T QUIT!

Another famous movie shows how you must get off of the canvas when you are all but out for the count. My hero, Rocky Balboa, shows us that we must rely upon our inner heart, or spirit, if we are to overcome the odds against us. Our opponent may be the odds-on favorite, but if we learn how to tap into that inner strength like Rocky did, some inspiration from within will lift us beyond what we think we can endure.

When I was drowning in life's miseries and each day brought the same scene, my fear was that I would become a bitter, depressed individual for the rest of my life.

And when I awoke as a new person I wasn't accustomed to, that fear intensified. It was the same sad feeling, the feeling of both helplessness and hopelessness. I questioned. I wondered. I feared the worst. I prayed whether I should go on.

When I was daily wallowing in my sorrow, one of our friends, Marcia, had the nerve to ask, "Have you thanked God for your current condition?"

My first thought was to go for her throat, and then I thought she was simply insane. At that time, I never thought I would be thanking God for that experience.

But this book's purpose is just that.

The victory in Christ Jesus is sweet. If just one soul can be spared from or aided in the deep, dark pain of being unprepared for the spiritual battle that awaits us all, then this book will have served His purpose.

I wanted to write this book back in the '80s. I wrote a chapter in the '90s. By November of 2005, I had finished eight chapters. In two months I (He) wrote the last nine chapters. I have to reiterate what Rush Limbaugh says daily, "Talent is on loan from God."

CONTENTS

1980'S PHOTO

Chuck, Michele, Rochelle, & Chuckie
Our family is our life and our life is our family.

CHAPTER 1

RUNNING ON EMPTY OR RUNNING FROM GOD?

Pride goes before destruction and haughtiness before a fall.
Proverbs 16: 18.

And to man He said, "Behold the fear of the Lord, that is wisdom, and to depart from evil is understanding. Job 28: 28.

Chances are you are reading this book to try to make some rhyme or reason from things that have occurred either in your life or the life of one of your loved ones that seemed too much to handle. Chances are you are wondering why your world collapsed; after all, you worked hard, always trying to do your best to keep it all together. And to your credit, you have chosen to work your way back. If this is a reason you have chosen to read this book, I hope that some of the words that you digest within this book offer you at least a seed of hope, a seed of belief, a seed of light, a seed to go on. My exact wishes for you are exactly what I did not possess during the summer of 1985.

Pope John Paul II said, "Nobody can undo what already has been done. Even the best psychologists cannot free us from our past. Only the omnipotence of God can do this." And that's exactly what I am about to share with you. After building my life's desires to a peak point, I saw God slowly but surely wipe away anything that would stand in the way of my love for Him. I realized the truth of what Sister Mora taught us back in the fifth grade at St. Mary's of Mentor: "God is good, for if He were to allow us to see (like viewing a movie) what life's experiences would bring, you would die on the spot from a massive heart attack."

Well, I felt like that when He gradually began to tear down all that I had built up. First, He took away my career, not just a job, but a position for which I had both a passion and purpose. Along with that went the company car, the executive benefits and health and life insurance for my family. Michele and I were just thirty-five, Rochelle was ten, and Chuck was eight years old. Even our small family business, Tommy Edwards Records, was in peril. As each day passed, I thought surely that the things occurring to my family were not just or fair from a loving God. I believed that He would restore me to the status I had worked so hard to achieve.

Well, you have heard the old saying, "Things went from bad to worse." After losing the worldly things and still trusting in Him, He began to dismantle my family. My wife filed for divorce. Then members of her family thought it best that I did not see my daughter and son for awhile, and the professionals to whom I had gone for help had no answers. God's next choice was my mind. That's right, He took that also. I was clinically depressed. And as every moment felt like an eternity, I began to doubt His promises. If He delivered what He said He would, why, why would he strip me of everything? What happened? What did I do to deserve such a fate?

In the movie *A Few Good Men* with Tom Cruise and Jack Nicholson, Nicholson was on the witness stand, and Cruise was grilling him with question after question. Cruise's last response wasn't a question. "I want the truth," he demanded. Nicholson reached his breaking point and blurted out, "Truth! You want the truth? You can't handle the truth!"

That's the exact position I found myself in for quite some time. I thought I knew the truth. I thought by living the truth, by being a man of my word, truth would prevail. I thought wrong. Although I did not know it at the time, I knew only the truth and wisdom of this world.

I was about to embark upon a journey that was far beyond what I as a mere man could weather, but it was a journey that would teach me the difference between human wisdom and divine wisdom. His plan was set for my de-programming. The one thing I can tell you from experience: the journey is tough, at times it seems impossible, but it's do-able! *I will never leave or forsake you.* Joshua 1:5.

In mid-June of 1985, involuntarily my whole world changed. I resigned from a prosperous vice presidency. But there was no golden parachute that is normal for an executive of ten years to receive. Instead, I felt as if I had been blindsided and pushed out the window with nothing to protect my fall. The only way to describe such an experience is to tell you to envision yourself a boxer. You're in the ring, you're working hard trying to survive the round, when BANG, your corner hits you in the back of the head with a brick.

When the going got rough at the company, instead of planning, setting mutual objectives and following our set goals together as we had done for over a decade, our owner decided to play the Lone Ranger. His sin was to try to conceal the truth by hiding behind someone who had made a career building upon truth. So, he chose to make me the sacrificial lamb, all without my knowledge. The credibility I had built up got him the time needed to camouflage the truth.

Another key factor that really hurt was that the owner was my wife's first cousin. Family was another part of life I thought I understood. I had a lot to learn. There was a lot of blame to go around. I was very proud of myself when it came to managing money. It's often said that timing is everything. My timing for moving our family into a brand new custom home couldn't have been worse. In today's money, we had over $200,000 in our savings account. My annual salary also approached $200,000 in 2006 money. You guessed it. I chose to put most of our savings into our new home, and less than six months later I had no job, benefits or future.

Images of my wife and my two children flashed before me. Worry set in on how I was going to keep the family together, pay the mortgage on our new home, keep the kids in private school, make the car payments and pay for health insurance. The list went on in my mind over and over again. So, my resignation also had guilt built in from what I viewed were my poor choices.

Please understand that this is not conduct I was accustomed to. After all, for me every goal set was attained. From being in danger of failing the second grade to receiving my MBA at age twenty-eight, from sweeping the truck docks in high school to being named a vice president at twenty-nine, from being a long-haired musician to becoming a distinguished military graduate and receiving an honorable discharge from the service as a Vietnam-era first lieutenant coming from a divorced family to being happily married— the list went on and on. QUIT. That word was unthinkable to me! "Relentless Persistence" is our daughter Rochelle's label for me. These might have been the two words most associated with how Chuck Rambaldo was put together. In retrospect, the three words that could describe my character were loyal, consistent and honest. These are the traits that built my reputation and made me a success in the business world. I parlayed my worldly achievements into raising a happy and healthy household. A beautiful wife, who shared my love of our children, and now a custom home we recently moved into. What more can a man ask for? It seemed I had achieved the American Dream.

After a decade as vice president of labor relations and human resources, I made a moral decision to walk away from a position I not only excelled in but also one that I had a true passion and gift for. I did not realize it at the time, but my priorities in life were totally out of sync.

How did I not see this coming, you ask? What happened to the "can do" attitude I had possessed since early childhood? And most important, where was my energy? Where was Mr. Charlie Hustle, the guy who worked sixty hours a week while overseeing our family retail music operation, attended graduate school three nights a week, served as a reserve officer every fourth weekend and worked with Michele to maintain our family life? I could hardly get out of bed!

Remember when I told you He began to dismantle all that I had built? Part of that was a choice or choices I had made over time not to listen to Him. He had been sending me messengers, but I had failed to hear His call! Only when I was on my back was I willing to look up! A neighbor, Jerry Wrobel, would try to "plant the seed" that I was missing something vital in life, but I just disregarded him. After all, he was one of those "born-agains". We all know they have emotional crutches. That's why they are like they are, I thought. But what he was offering I had no knowledge of. I just feared it.

When Michele and I were taking Bible study from our pastor at St. Rita's Church of Solon, he tried to fluff off the term of "born-again" by saying. "Yeah, I'm a born-again. Every day I wake up, I am born again." How silly, I thought. This was from the mouth of my spiritual leader? It took me years to understand how simple it really is. We are first born from our mother's womb (flesh), and then we MUST BE born again—from above—spiritually.

After attaining all the goals I set, I was not prepared for the emotional drain that devoured my mind, body, and soul. What I did on that fateful morning was a result of what had most likely been occurring in my life for quite some time.

By now, you have all heard of the sad story in American business of what happened at ENRON! I experienced a similar business fate in the summer of 1985. As we all know, the closer to the fire you are, the more apt you are to get burned. I was right next to the source of the inferno. The owner, my mentor, had a life-choice decision to make and decided to try to deflect the heat on me. I was left to make a decision I never envisioned, one involving ethics and morals. A position I could not fix: a position I could never imagine anyone knowingly placing another in.

I'll never forget the vice president of finance's words: "Just sell the workers on this bullshit, and you know that company car you're driving? Those paid vacations? You know that nice salary with the corporate perks? All of us officers will still have them ten years from now BUT those poor bastards down in the factory... They're f-----! This plant will be a ghost town in less than 90 days!" I walked out of his office dumbfounded and numb. I kept replaying his words over and over: "The workers are f-----. We'll still have ours in ten years."

The individual I needed to talk to, the owner, was conveniently out of the country. For the first time in my life, I could not come up with a solution. For the first time in my life, I could not believe such a choice could be made by an individual that I trusted, believed in and one who portrayed himself to be a man of his word. He deliberately chose—and I am sure it was a difficult choice to make, yet he did choose it—to put my head in a vice. The company where I had worked for a decade had grown from one plant and 250 employees to five plants and over 1,500 employees. The Accurate Die Casting Company was featured in *Machine and Tool Blue Book Magazine* as a model of how to treat employees. (See Appendix.) This publication was widely read and respected in the industry. However, Accurate Die Casting was about to implode. Remember, all the goals I had set I attained. For the past few years at Accurate Die Casting, I lived out of a suitcase to try to save the company. I was the heat shield, the firewall. I was the individual who worked tirelessly to try to make management and labor get along. All in vain.

On top at thirty-five years old, and the next day hardly alive might have been the way you could have described me. It hit me that morning. My corporate business career was over. How could that be? All my life I relied on the principle, Be a man of your word. I was. It worked for me—until now. Now, by relying on that principle, I was about to lose it all—career, financial security, health, both physical and mental and soon, family. Is that fair? Is that just? Or is that just —life?

So, on that dark and dreary day as I ever so slowly tried to get out of bed, gone was the feeling of "Up and at 'em! Let's get to it! There is much to accomplish today." The vision of what the day would bring was no vision at all! As I sat on the edge of the bed, a totally different feeling engulfed me. I had no physical energy. I had no mental energy. I had absolutely no spiritual energy. I was beginning to realize something. I was out of fuel. I WAS RUNNING ON EMPTY! I was also running from God.

My mind began to rewind. It seems we always wonder how did we get in such a position after we are deep in it! Only if… I was drifting back…only if…Back to my early childhood days when things were…Well, they weren't so great then either.…

Rick and Chuck enjoying a family event with their cousins

Rick and Chuck dressed to the nines, even when working.
Now that's Italian!

CHAPTER 2

FAMILIA: THE FAMILY

Wherever your treasure is, there your heart and thoughts will be also. Luke 12: 34.

He shall give you the desires of your heart. Psalms 37: 4.

In case you didn't know it, we Italians are a very proud people. Our culture does almost everything to excess—eat, celebrate, love and hate. We are also very proud of what part of "the country" our families are from. When I was young, that's all I heard at family gatherings. Italian-Americans, when they meet another kinsman, are also interested to know where your people are from in Italy. Where is your mom's family from? How about your pop's *familia*? I only knew Willoughby and Little Italy. As it turns out, our mom's "people" came from Abrruzzese. Dad's people came from Napoletanoa (Naples), and according to our dad, Abrruzzese stands for "hardheads."

I must share with you that the title of this book stems from what I feel most Italian men were brought up to be—men of their word. A handshake was a binding contract. That was before society was run by legalism and the mindset that if you really want an agreement, you'd better get it in writing. We were also taught that when you opened your mouth, you meant every word that was coming out of it. Now, it seems there is a "gimme" rule. Most people are accustomed to "gimme a break." Do you really expect everyone to abide by what they say? You are naïve enough to expect others to abide by the rules and the law? Get real!

I would like to share my family with you to enlighten you as to how I was (humanly) constructed. In her early years, Mom was unlike her parents and siblings. On more than one occasion, I have suggested to her that maybe she was adopted. They were Italian immigrants, happy with the plain and ordinary. Not Mom! She had flair! She loved the new and unusual, and both were becoming to her. She graduated from the prestigious Andrews School for Girls in Willoughby, Ohio, in 1942. This is a source of lifelong source of pride for her.

She was born Mary Ann Pascieulo. But she loved the name of one of her aunts, Neddie, and at some point in her life simply took it as her own. In fact, years later when our parents decided to "live the American dream" and operate their own business in 1957, it was her name that went up in lights! Neddie's Beverage became a gathering place in beautiful Eastlake, Ohio.

Mom's family was very musical. Her father, Angelo, and her mother, Lucy, did not possess such talent, but both of her brothers, John and Arnold, were talented musicians. Our Uncle John was the jokester. Mom says I got my quick wit from him. I learned he didn't joke all the time. When he asked you to do something for him, you should comply. He once asked me if I loved him. "Of course" was my reply. "Then," he said, "take our neighbor's granddaughter to her prom. She doesn't have a date."

I declined. "I don't even know the girl, and you want me to take her to her prom?"

He retorted that if I wanted him to talk to me, I would reconsider and take the girl. I did! Now, that's Italian negotiating!

He used to take Rick and me to his garden in his Frazer—a car that would stall and the right door would swing wide open when he made a left-hand turn. Of course, this was before seat belts. Uncle John would always reach across the seat to keep Rick and me from hitting the front dash. In those days, the dashes were made of metal. Ouch!

My mom's only sister, my Aunt Laura, was a lot like her mother. She truly enjoyed being at home with her family. She was all of four feet, eight inches, while Uncle Andy was well over six feet tall. Aunt Laura and her two children, Andrea and Joey, lived close to Little Italy. So, in the days of family gatherings in Willoughby, they would drive Route 20. There were no freeways yet. After a fun Sunday with them, Rick and I gave Joey a Davy Crockett coonskin hat.

Fearing his father's reaction, Joe chose to put it on only when his family arrived in their driveway. Joe tells us his father looked in the rear view mirror and asked. "Joe, where did you get that hat?"

"Cousin Rick and Chook," he replied.

He said his dad did not say another word.

He simply put the car in reverse and drove all the way back to Willoughby to drop the hat off. Now, that's Italian!

Uncle Arnold, on the other hand, appeared quieter and more reserved. Yet, he might have been the only true rebel in the family, aside from Neddie, that is. He was a barber, trumpet player, owner of a Harley-Davidson motorcycle, driver of a little Nash Rambler and recipient of a Purple Heart for his fighting in World War II. When our children were young, Uncle Arnold and my father-in-law would play music in our home in Twinsburg. Not only did he leave me great musical memories, but he also shared them with my kids.

He experienced a lot of the bad parts of life and had a lot of mean and rotten things done to him but never seemed to complain. After he had a nervous breakdown from flashbacks over being injured in a tank in World War II, his wife left him and took his baby daughter, Lorrianne. He passed away unexpectedly in 1984, just ninety days after my dad.

Uncle Arnold chose to endure the hardships of life. He is one of my few heroes. I used to borrow his record-making machine, and

Gary Borrelli and I recorded "Louie, Louie," "Hang on Sloopy," and "Gloria" when they were climbing the charts. I wish I had those self-made records now.

Speaking of Gary, we were best of buds in the eighth grade back at good ole St. Mary's. Gary was almost like family. My home was always open for band practices. I named our group Tossed Salad. Well, one spring Friday, I was talking to Gary when I shouldn't have been during Sister Theklas' class. She stopped her instruction at the chalkboard. "Mr. Borrelli, if I hear one word out of your mouth the rest of this afternoon, and I will come back there and stuff this chalk rag in your mouth for the rest of the day. Do you hear me?"

Well, a few minutes later, I was taunting him. "Gary, she doesn't mean it. What time should I come over tonight?"

Poor Gary's second mistake was to tell me, "Be quiet, Ram..."

That is as far as he got. "Mr. Borrelli," Sister Thekla proclaimed. She began walking down the aisle towards our seats in the rear of the class. "Mr. Borrelli, open your mouth." "No, Sister, I was..."

She interrupted him mid-sentence and stuffed the chalky rag into his mouth. Gary, if you're out there, thanks for taking the rap for me. I am truly sorry.

Not much later in the school year, I got mine. The same nun asked me to give a progress report on the Red Cross drive I was collecting money for from the class. When I asked her to give me a day to prepare the paperwork, she replied, "Now, mister."

Being the independent spirit that I am, I put in a second request and boldly informed her that no way would I give a report that day.

She took her wooden pointer and used it on my back and shoulders. End result. She took out her frustrations, and I held my ground.

The family gatherings at the Paschull (their Italian name had been legally changed from Pascieulo) household in Willoughby were times I fondly remember. Both uncles played away on their accordions, and everyone joined in singing, telling family stories and laughing. To this day, Mom starts her day with a song. She always has the radio tuned into her favorite station. Mom has a God-given musical talent herself. She is a natural dancer. She has rhythm. Mom, over the years, has repeatedly told us the story of how a well-known dancer, Carlos, asked her to become part of his TV dancing team. When she refused, the dancing duo became Carlos and Kay.

Mom loved Louis Prima. She will still tell the story of how she went to the Palace Theatre in downtown Cleveland on a bus when she was six months pregnant just to see Louis Prima play. She would often rock both of us to Louis's tune of "Oh Babe." If you have ever listened to Louis' tempo of music, you know why Rick and I, at times, can be a little hyper. I think that's why Louis is one of my favorite artists. This guy may not have been a part of the famous and fabulous Rat Pack, but he combined all forms of music—big band, jazz, Dixieland, swing, rock, duets and comedy.

That's our Mom. A real free spirit, and a real gift to both of her children and to her grandchildren. I got my love of music from Mom's side of the family. By the grace of God, she and I still work together in the music field. I, too, loved to dance, and Mom encouraged me to take drum lessons. I was sure I'd be the next Gene Krupa. My only true claim to fame was that one of my drum instructors, Denny Benson, went on to record with Cleveland's own Outsiders of "Time Won't Let Me" fame. Ironically, I played with a group called The Flock at Andrews School for Girls, Mom's alma mater, for their prom in 1968. To be honest, my earliest memories of Mom are those of having a nice loving home, of her working hard in the store, Neddie's Beverage, to help support my brother and me and her gentle way of showing us how a parent and a person of outstanding character tries to live life.

Both of our parents shared the belief that actions speak louder than words, a concept I have lived by throughout my life. I can never remember being spanked or actually hit by either of our parents. Come to think of it, I don't recall them ever embarrassing us either. Their "look" or their words were enough to make us get the message.

Mom's involvement in my life is even more meaningful during my later years, and I will explain this in later chapters.

Our dad, on the other hand, left me with some very vivid and specific memories, especially in my childhood. One of them involved a scary incident at a family picnic around 1958. I was eight years old and my brother Rick nine. It is the only family function that I can recall with both sides of the family participating, both Mom's side and Dad's. He was an excellent swimmer and loved the water. He used to show off for us kids. Once, while we were on vacation, he was showing off how he could do a handstand under water. Remember, this was in the '50s when Italian men were supposed to be macho. We were impressed with our dad's ability to perform such tricks for us. He was really entertaining. But when it came time to drive back to the motel in our snazzy '55 Chevy—no keys! Where could they be? Seems Grumpie had lost the keys at the bottom of the lake while he was performing his upside-down water maneuvers, pumping his feet in the air. Grumpie was his nickname for he rarely cracked a smile; after all, he was working three jobs: as a machinist, as a landscaper and as a small business owner of Neddie's Beverage.

On the day at the family picnic, he was going to teach his sons to swim and also all of our cousins—Marilyn, Andrea, Joey, and Karen. To this day, we all share a family bond of that blessed event at Tuttle Park in Madison, Ohio. The bond is that of fear and terror you can only relate to if you have been in water over your head. For, you see, my dad's method of instruction in the way to tread water was to toss us into the water that was over our heads. He figured our own survival instincts would eventually kick in, and we would swim like fish.

When I think about it even now, I can feel that strange sensation of "Water, water, everywhere! And a lot to drink!" I can still visualize him taking both of us, one on each shoulder, to water that was around his chest and promptly throwing Rick in first since he was the oldest. After a while, Rick was not doing what he was supposed to. So, Dad threw me in to rescue son number one. Needless to say, he had two drowning children on his hands. He was a man of action and intuitively grabbed Rick first with his right hand since he was under the longest. Then he reached down and grabbed me up from the depths with his left hand. He calmly carried us both back to shore. He never really admitted his method might not be the right one, but it was supposed to work. He had witnessed it done with success.

I recently read in the newspaper that an eyewitness to a horrific event can recall it exactly as it happened even twenty years later. I'll give a big amen to that. I wish I could erase it from my mind, for I have tried over the years unsuccessfully. It stays as vivid as if it were yesterday. And to this day, none of the six of us who were there that day for our first swimming lesson can swim!

Another memory I wish I could erase was the day Rick and I discovered blood coming from under the upstairs bathroom door in Willoughby, Ohio. Thank God, we shot downstairs and got help from our older cousin, JoAnn. She knew enough to keep us from further viewing the scene. We did not understand until sometime later what had happened—that our Uncle Arnold was depressed and had slit his wrists.

Sometimes family means well, but the end results are life-lasting

29

impressions that are not always positive in nature. When they say opposites attract, that's a pretty accurate analysis of our mom and dad. Rick and I would not have chosen anyone else to be our father and our mother, but husband and wife? Frank and Mary Ann were a combustible pair. I believe that they each truly thought they knew what was right for the situation at hand, but as the other old saying goes "No man can serve two masters." Both of our parents were strong-willed individuals. Both of them wanted to be the head of the house, and back in those days, that was a given for most men.

Dad sort of married out of his league, and he paid a price for it. Mom, in retrospect, most probably married beneath herself, and she, too, paid a price for that. And Rick and I paid a price for their paying a price. I can recall attending family gatherings after their split, and things did change. I remember, at a very young age, making a conscious decision never to marry an Italian lady. In doing an analysis of the families, it appeared to me that most of my relatives had married Italians and most had either divorced or remained "together for the kids."

I remember telling my dad, who wanted Rick and me to be priests, that I would never marry. The other belief I possessed was that if I did marry, I would do that for life. Probably this was because of the experience I felt from my parents' divorce.

One last story about my parents' divorce. After the divorce, our dad took an active interest in our lives. He was the one who took Rick and me on the few vacations of our youth. He took us everywhere he went. One local place he went was the Forest Hills Bowling Alley. Rick and I were about fourteen and fifteen years old, and as we walked into Forest Hills Lanes one time, there, dressed in hoodlum garb, was our cousin, Joe Comai. He saw us, sort of waved but did not come over to us. Dad looked at the appearance of friends he was with, and I could tell he was concerned for Joe's choice.

Dad motioned for Joey to come over to us. When he did, he said, "Hi, Rick. Hi, Chuck. Hi, Frank."

Dad did not lose a second. "What did you call me?"

Joe repeated, "Frank."

"Frank ? Who told you to say that?"

Joe replied, "My parents." Then my dad said something I thought was very profound. "Listen, Joe, you may not understand what transpired between your Aunt Neddie and myself, but you're still my nephew and I'm still your uncle. Get it?"

"Yeah, Uncle Frank, I do."

Then Dad tried to give him another lesson in life. "Joe, you know, I grew up with some of those guys' fathers you're hanging around with. They are not people you should associate with. Joe, you have to make a decision. Stick with your cousins and bowl a few games with us."

Joe tipped the bad-guy hat he was wearing, and simply said, "See ya."

The title of this book has a little to do with our father and his being a man of his word. Let me tell you, just because he never hit us nor embarrassed us, he said what he meant and he meant what he said. He did not choose his words lightly. I can never recall him acting differently from what he professed from his mouth.

Having only one brother, I might be expected to have a lot to share when it came to growing up with Brother Rick. Well, you're right. I originally had written my Top Ten Escapades with Brother Rick! I had to dwindle them down to four escapades, and the first is simply entitled JAIL! In our father's talk on the steps in Mentor before the divorce, he listed three main commandments of his own: No lying.

No stealing. And his primo point was No JAIL! Well, Rick got a chance to test our father on that part.

‣Escapade Number One: JAIL

To Rick's credit, he was working his tail off to make monthly payments on his car. And, as the story goes, one night just after work, he was showing a few of his buddies how he could "peel rubber". Wouldn't you know it? One of those fine men in blue happened to witness this and brought Rick into the police station. I guess it's against the law to do that.

Well, the phone rang late that same evening at Grandma Rambaldo's house where we lived in the summer. I picked it up, and, to my surprise, Rick did not sound like the confident brother he normally was.

"Chuck?" He almost whispered.

"Rick, is that you? Is everything all right?"

"Get Dad up. I'm being detained in the Willowick police…" That's all I had to hear… "…for peeling. He has to come down and sign for me to get out."

"Rick, do you remember what he told us about going to jail?"

"Aw, you don't believe that stuff, do you? Besides, this is not the same thing."

Well, I apprehensively walked across the hall to our dad's bedroom and turned on his lights. "Rick's on the phone," I said, "and there is some small misunderstanding. He is down at the police station…."

That's as far as I got. "Police station?" He erupted. "What did I tell you and your brother if you ever went to jail?"

"Well, Dad, this isn't quite the same thing…"

"Jail is jail," he proclaimed. "Now shut off the lights. I have to get up very early to go to work. And tell your brother to call his mother."

As I turned back to the phone, I was wondering how I was going to break the news to Rick. "Rick?"

"Yeah, what did he say?"

"What he told us about this situation years ago. 'Tell the police officer that your dad died the day you were born and call your mother.' I know Rick was in disbelief, but when it came to his two sons, Dad was a man of his word.

•Escapade Number Two: Summer Camp

The last memory of Grove Avenue was that it was summertime, and our dad thought it best we learn to mingle with other children. Rick and I were sort of shy and kept to ourselves. So, our parents had arranged for us to spend a few weeks away from home at summer camp. On the morning of the excursion, we were told to catch the bus at the local schoolyard. As we approached the schoolyard, we could see the buses and the kids getting on them.

Suddenly my brother blurted out, "Get in the bushes."

"What?"

"Yeah, we'll hide, miss the bus and tell our parents what happened."

I did not think it a good idea, but after all, he was one year, one month, and one day older than I. After we watched the school buses drive off, we calmly went home.

When our dad arrived home sometime later, he was shocked to see us there. "What are you doing home?"

"We missed the bus," Rick explained.

"Missed the bus, huh? Get in the car!" Yeah, Mr. Wisdom probably had figured out our scheme. He drove us to the camp, which was somewhere in Pennsylvania. Did that stop us? I think not. When my brother and I would not do the things the other children were doing like playing volleyball, swimming, trail hiking, the camp director called our parents. Who do you think drove all the way back up there to pick us up? Any verbal or physical assaults? Nope!

•Escapade Number Three: Superman

Then there was the time when Rick and I were watching the popular TV show *Superman*. All of a sudden he proclaimed, "I can do that. Watch me!" He calmly took the pillowcase off of one of the pillows on the bed, tied it around his neck and walked down the long hallway on the second floor of our home in Willoughby. I stood there in amazement as my brother proclaimed, "I can fly!" He began to run towards me as I stood in the doorway to the bedroom. He was flapping his hands as he approached take-off. All of a sudden, he came to a complete stop. The second floor window was closed. That did not deter him. He used his superpowers of calmness once again, opened the window and climbed out on top of the enclosed porch. Turning to me, he said "Look up in the sky and you will seem me soaring soon." So, being the trusting little brother, I fixed my eyes on the sky. He ran down the roof line, flapping his hands, and as I anxiously awaited take-off, he dropped out of sight! The next thing I heard was Rick moaning on the ground. His guardian angel must have been on his shoulder that day, for he simply limped away with a strained ankle and a bruised ego.

•Escapade Number 4: Mr. Baseball

Then there was the time I went to watch my older brother on his way to becoming a Mentor baseball legend. He was the starting center fielder. His team, the Phillies, was winning going into the bottom of the last inning. I can still see the pitch, the swing and— oh, no—the duck! That's right, the guy up to bat hit a high popper to—where else? Center field. I knew, I just knew my brother would be the hero and catch the final out. As gravity had its way with the baseball, I looked to my dismay and saw, along with everyone else in the crowd, my brother use his mitt for protection. He folded both of his arms over his head as the ball dropped harmlessly to the ground, and the runners scurried around the bases for the winning run. Result: Game over! The only other memory after that was the very next game. Rick got all suited up. He looked real good. We walked down to the park, and at the last moment he said, "Let's get in the bushes." I seem to recall we had done that somewhere else.

The memories of both of our parents are superb. Even though we grew up in an age where divorce was taboo, our divorced parents worked hard at being in every chapter of our lives. I am sure that their sacrifice was a road map that paved the way for both Rick and me when it came to raising our own children. And I am eternally grateful for that.

I know now how hard it truly is to stay the course when it comes to raising your own children. I think that is why at our daughter's wedding, part of my "father's speech" evolved from the example of my parents. My generation had a better chance, though, at making some serious bucks, and I did. But when it came to "selling out" That wasn't in my DNA. I told Mat, our son-in-law that as Mrs. Rambaldo and I worked together over the years, people would ask us, "What are you investing in?" My reply was simple. "Our children." And what a return on our investment they have given us!

1967
Chuck and his dad standing by Chuck's first classic car
'60 Dodge

1965
100 Dartmoor , our childhood home in Mentor, Ohio

CHAPTER 3

DAD'S WORDS OF WISDOM

A good name is to be more desired than great wealth. Proverbs 22: 1,

We have all fallen short of the glory of God. Romans 5: 12.

Well, to give our father his "props," in today's language, I have to inform you of some very positive things our dad did for Rick and me. We all have fond memories of growing up. It could be something we did, something we saw or something someone said to us. Some of these memories last a lifetime.

Let me tell you another childhood memory that was to be part of the groundwork and the foundation of the man I would become. On a fairly warm summer day, Dad took my brother and me outside on the front step for what was to become "the talk". Dad was always planting words of wisdom in our brains. He never minced his words; he always got straight to the point.

The point this particular time was when he told both of us that he and Mom were getting a divorce! Please remember that back in the '60s that word was taboo, especially for a child growing up in an Italian Catholic family. We weren't really old enough to realize it at the time, but Dad was about to sow seeds of wisdom (man's) into our souls with his words that day. He was a man, who though small in stature, commanded respect. He worked three jobs to support our family. His hands were calloused from hard labor, but he was always clean-shaven, tanned, and proud of his appearance. His voice was loud, even when he whispered, and as raspy as if he had chronic laryngitis. God had given him a stereotypical voice of "the Godfather."

"Stick out your hands," he told my brother. Instantly Rick obeyed.

Dad made a cutting gesture on Rick's wrists as if to visibly display what he was about to say.

"If you steal, I'll cut your hand off." Wow! That got our attention.

He then turned to me. "Stick out your tongue!" he ordered. I did.

"Lie, and I'll cut your tongue out. If you're not a man of your word, you're not a man. You're nothing." This when he threw in for good measure, "If either of you ever go to jail, you tell them that your dad died the day you were born. I will never embarrass our family name, and I expect both of you boys to follow suit."

Then he did mention that the divorce had nothing to do with us. He said that our mom was a good person, but that they just couldn't see eye to eye.

Rick and I sat on the front steps of our home in beautiful Mentor, Ohio, soaking in all that he had said to us. It was almost more than our young minds could absorb. But in my life's experiences, when push came to shove, when life threw me some unexpected curves, his words echoed in my mind over and over.

That summer I was about to enter the fifth grade at St. Mary's grade school. My real Christian name is Francis, named after my father. Quite unusual for the second-born son in a thoroughbred Italian family to be named for the father. By thoroughbred I mean that both parents are of the same nationality. However, Mom, the free spirit, was enamored with the name of a popular singer our parents had met in Canada. Thus, when my older brother was born, he was named Rick. When I was born, Dad finally got his namesake. Kids, as we all know, can be the worst tormentors. Despite my good nature, I often resented their jokes about a character that appeared at one of the fine department stores in downtown Cleveland, Francis, the talking mule. If you were fortunate enough to have the male name Francis, you might also have been teased with "Is that Frances with an E?" With an E, you see, was the way you spelled the girl's name. But at home, because of my hearty appetite, I grew into a chubby little boy. My family nicknamed me Chooky, which was Italian for chubby. More than once I have heard the story of how I ate from a tablespoon when I was only three weeks old. Mom, like most Italian mothers, thinks food is the cure-all for anything that ails you. I used to tease our kids that Situ Dolly, as they affectionately called her, should have opened a diner and called it Let's Eat.

One day I had forgotten my lunch money, and my dad came to school and knocked on my classroom door. Mr. Green cracked the door open a bit to answer his knock. A deep gravelly voice could be heard throughout the classroom as he inquired whether a "Chooky" Rambaldo was in this class. My teacher replied that, indeed, there was a Francis Rambaldo.

The voice answered, "Yeah, that's him. Give him this money for his lunch, will you?"

Of course, my snooty little friends loved this. "Chooky, Chooky," they sang out in whispers around my desk. I had to think quickly. This might be the first trial where my Uncle John's wit came in handy. It was get creative or be further humiliated with another name for them to tease me with. "What does that mean?" They kept prodding. "Chooky is Italian for Chuck. Yeah, Chuck's my nickname," I told them, ever the diplomat.

There I sat, waiting for what seemed to be a lifetime for their collective response. To my surprise and delight, they admired the name. I came to be Chuck to all of my schoolyard friends from that day forth, just like my mom, Mary Ann, had become Neddie for the rest of her life.

I hated the divorce. I was just ten years old. Most of those ten years, I had spent trying to be the family peacemaker. I was always busy trying to make my parents laugh. I thought if they laughed at me, they were getting along with each other. Once I faced the fact that our dad was not home every day, I felt an unspeakable pain as a result. It is not something that can be defined. I believe that only children who experience divorce at a young age can know that similar pain. I know now that I am grateful for the experiences that came out of the shared custody between my parents. Dad insisted that he would continue to provide the lifestyle to which his family had become accustomed by allowing Mom to keep the nice house where Rick and I were already settled in school and had friends. There we were part of an upscale community and lived in a well-groomed, middle-class neighborhood.

We had our hair cut to school code and wore neat, clean uniforms according to the dictates of the school. Life was regimented, predictable and afforded a sense of continuity, which made our transition into the single-parent situation easier. There were no threats to our identity, and we didn't have to struggle to prove ourselves. Life went on as usual…during the school year, at least. Another lesson Dad gave us in "the talk," was about worldly things. He said, "You see this nice house, nice neighborhood, new car and small business we own? They mean nothing if you don't have an inner peace and peace within your family."

Remember, if you ever find yourselves in a similar circumstance, let go of these things. You can always buy them back, but you can't buy peace of mind or your family's love.

When summer arrived, there was a 180-degree turn-around. Rick and I packed up and left the cozy comforts of the suburbs to live at our paternal Grandmother Mary's home with our dad in East Cleveland. It really didn't dawn on me until much later in life how hard that must have been for our father to pack up and rent from his mother. Now, East Cleveland in the mid-'60s was almost comparable to the image some people have of the Bronx. This neighborhood and its ethnic element of rivalry were to become a part of the fiber of my life. Yet, it was nothing short of a blessing that took us there. Rick and I had the taste of both worlds with this arrangement. We became book smart in a wonderful school system where learning was truly the focus. And we became street smart with lots of "bad boys" from the Murray Hill district of Little Italy, as Grandma's neighborhood in Cleveland was often referred to. To give you an example of the different life experiences, our home in Mentor offered the finest in baseball diamonds, beautiful tree-lined streets to ride our bikes on in safety and a back yard as big as a football field where Rick and I could play baseball or football. Back then, no American boy was playing soccer!

East Cleveland, on the other hand, left me with an experience only worthy to be told in this book. I should sub-chapter it with the title, I Wrestled with Rats.

One night I came home from a date with Michele, a bit after my curfew. Does anyone still use that word? I must have been seventeen years old. Grandma Mary had been the wife of an abusive Italian alcoholic, while raising three children alone. Let me tell you, when Grandma Mary said something, you'd better be listening. She was not an easy woman to reckon with at any hour, let alone the wee hours of the morning. So, I took my shoes off before coming in the front door. But, alas, I knew she was up and about because I could hear her crunching and munching her favorite cereal, Special K. Bravely, I tiptoed down the hall to face the music.

As I timidly peeked around the corner, what a shock I got! Sitting on top of the kitchen table was a huge pack rat. Please don't get the wrong picture. This was no ordinary field mouse or small rodent. This guy towered over the cereal box he had chewed into. He was totally at home in this neighborhood and inside our house. He simply turned his head, stared at me for a moment, and then resumed his meal. Needless to say, I slept in the bathroom that night because it was the only room in the house with a lock on it.

We have all heard the words, "Life's a choice." And sometimes, as difficult as it may be, it's true. Our dad chose, and I am sure it was not an easy choice, to be the father he never had. My father's father, Louie, was a man I only recall seeing once in my life. When Rick and I were teenagers, for some reason, Dad wanted us to meet our grandfather. He lived in Detroit, Michigan. When Dad drove us up there, the image I still see was Grandpa standing in front of a beer joint, a place where I never saw my dad. By the time we parked the car, he was gone.

Louie was an alcoholic, an abusive individual, both verbally and physically. He once tied our father to a tree when he was a boy to show him his version of punishment. He was a deadbeat dad. Things got so bad for our grandmother that she had to have the "powers that be" in Little Italy give Louie an ultimatum. Leave town or die!

By the time Grandma Mary was twenty-one, she was left to raise three children with no husband, let alone alimony or child support. Dad had to quit Murray High School in the ninth grade to try to help support the family. Unlike his father, our dad chose another path in raising his two boys. He never belittled us or even hit us once. His strength with his kids was in his character.

On more than one occasion, Dad would take Rick and me to Little Italy's Feast in Murray Hill, the town he grew up in. All of his childhood friends would be sitting on chairs outside in tailored suits and groomed to the nines. Remember, our dad was a blue-collar worker, who at times was working three jobs. When we asked him why they all weren't working, he simply replied, "I grew up with these guys, but I choose not to hang with them." Then he said something very profound. "For what you hang around with you become like." As Proverbs 13:30 says, *He who walks with wise men will be wise, but the companion of fools will suffer harm.*

Let me say that I am well aware that Dad was a sinner and that parts of his character were flawed. He also "wrestled with demons" and suffered from depression at times. He was a mere man, after all. When it came to reprimanding us kids, he was normally a man of few words. He had told us what was the right thing to do, and he expected us to do it. He was a man of his word, and he expected his sons to be the same.

In his book, *Big Russ and Me*, my fellow classmate at John Carroll University, the late Tim Russert, is asking his father if he was tempted to take money in a certain situation. His father's reply was, "Like I said, it wasn't the right thing to do. And how could I tell you kids to do the right thing if I ever did something like that?"

Russert continues, "That story means the world to me. At the time, Dad was sending two or three kids to parochial school, paying the mortgage, and working two jobs, but he held his ground. Others didn't do the right thing, and Dad didn't get the promotion, but he kept his honor."

Tim also clears up what was somewhat of a puzzle to me. Back in 1970, four Kent State students were killed on campus by the National Guard. I was in R.O.T.C. at the time, and there was a division about this between the long-haired radicals and the short-haired conservatives. I can recall the chaos Tim speaks of at John Carroll at that time. Tim was president of our student union. At first, he appeared to have lost it and was speaking out against the war and anyone who was a part of it. I took offense to that. I thought the young men in Vietnam were dying for our country, and who were we to judge them? The war was not popular, but why condemn those that are serving their country?

Tim seemed to have a changed attitude over a brief period. I never understood it until three-and-one-half decades later I read, "That night [of the Kent State shootings], I called home. 'Dad they're killing us,' I said. 'No, a guardsman may have lost his head, but they're not trying to kill you.' His voice was firm. What he couldn't tolerate were television images of protestors spitting on Vietnam Veterans, carrying the Viet Cong flag.

Tim wrote, "When I returned to school in the fall, I found myself repeating what Dad had said and drawing the line between protest and patriotism: We can be for peace without supporting the enemy. We can be against this war without rooting for the other side."

It is evident to me that there were many fathers planting their seeds of wisdom at that time. Tim's reaction to his book about his dad was to write another one, sharing the wisdom of our fathers.

If our dad said he was picking us up on the weekend, he was always there. And he planned his weekends around us. His kids were his life. I can recall many Friday evenings he would drive all the way from work, pick us up and drive us back from the far eastern suburb of Mentor to East Cleveland. This was all before freeways. I still remember the fear I felt sometimes on those trips because Dad was so exhausted that Ricky would have to steer the car and wake Dad as each red light turned green.

He didn't seem to regret that he had to quit school in the ninth grade to help his mother support the family. His sisters, Cora and Jean, were younger. Tragically, Jean died as a child after being hit by a Red Ball truck. He seldom let the forces of life get him down. He eventually went on to finish high school by earning a GED and even attended college at nights when he was in his fifties. He was so proud of that achievement that he invited me to sit in on one of his evening classes. After listening to him engage in dialogue with the professor, I knew that if he had been given different circumstances in life, only God knows how far he could have gone.

Dad was human and had times of sadness and depression, as I have mentioned. But I learned from him as I saw him make opportunities out of his struggles. He became a night supervisor in his forties, and in his sixties, he was head groundskeeper of a local cemetery. In his sixty-four years of life (1919-1983), he continuously tried to be a man of his word. And his words were not merely superficial as a means to an end. His word was his bond. You could always depend on it. His words were supportive, never demeaning, ridiculing, or cutting. His words were kind and caring, yet forceful, firm, and fair.

In Tim Russert's words, "The best sermons in life are lived, not spoken." That seems to be what our fathers' generation did. They walked the walk. Their actions spoke louder than words.

1960
Chuck and brother Rick
This was his first mass as an altar boy!

CHAPTER 4

IN THE NAME OF THE FATHER, SON, AND WHO?

But when the Holy Spirit comes upon you, you will receive the power to testify about me with great effort And to the ends of the earth. Acts 1: 8.

But the Comforter, which is the Holy Spirit, whom the Father will send in my name, he shall teach you all things and bring to your remembrance all that I have said to you. John 14: 26.

May I tell you about my early involvement with the church? Don't misconstrue my meaning. I am glad my parents had foresight to see that my brother and I were raised with a Christian upbringing.

My earliest recollections of my faith training begin at 100 Dartmoor Avenue in Mentor, Ohio. Rick and I have such fond memories about these times that we both bring our families back every now and then to let them see our childhood home. Somehow, they don't seem to share the enjoyment Rick and I get from these trips.

One cold and very dark winter morning my brother and I were brought back into the world when the lights went on in the bedroom we shared. Mom was waking us up. We were lucky enough to be the altar boys of the week at St. Mary's Mentor. This meant a 5:30 a.m. taxicab ride.

To our parents' credit, they both agreed to sacrifice and give us the best education money could buy. Back in those days, boys had to learn Latin to become members of the elite servers club. And learn we did. I don't honestly think I got anything spiritual out of it, but it was good training for life. There was Father Druher, our pastor; Father Permi, who left the Catholic Church to get married, and Father Steil, who liked Rick to pour all the wine into the cup and just a drop of water from me. But partaking of the spirits at 6:00

a.m.? I guess he required something extra to get him started. At that hour of the morning, we saw the usual crowd—two or maybe three ladies in their babushkas.

I received a better enlightenment on religion than my parents. In retrospect, we were taught Baltimore Catechism; little tiny minds absorbed whatever information was put in the rules of the game of life and Christianity. It was great for my first thirty-five years, but when the world betrayed me, it was inadequate to anchor me for the storm. I had heard our nuns and priests mention The Holy Spirit, (back then we called Him the Holy Ghost) who was simply depicted as a picture of a white dove. At thirty-five, I was physically and mentally an adult, but spiritually I was back at St. Mary's grade school in Mentor. In my infinite wisdom, I thought I was prepared to fight the good fight; after all, I had received more than nineteen years of a strong Christian foundation, educated with an MBA from John Carroll University, and I was the dutiful husband and father who led by example.

We all know the old saying, "Actions speak louder than words." For the first thirty-five years of my life, I let my actions do the talking, and this worked well for me. But I was sadly mistaken about my abilities to withstand the darkness of this world. In making the sign of the cross, we recite, "In the name of The Father, and of The Son and of The Holy Spirit." I knew The Father had created me, and The Son had died for me, but who was this Holy Spirit?

Now, in my fifties, I truly realize He is the key to a sustained and peaceful life. It was at Pentecost that Jesus offered us the Comforter. When you accept Jesus Christ as your Lord and Savior, you are born again. This is a term that sometimes frightens us Catholics. I know it did me! This is true because a major part of the Catholic teachings falls short of bringing us to the real altar of Christ. It was through His shed blood on the Cross that we are offered salvation. It is by the gifts of the Holy Spirit that we are allowed to understand more fully the spiritual side of life. It is through Him that we become a new creation in Christ.

It is my wish that many of us Catholics tap into the divine power of the Holy Spirit before we are shipwrecked. I know it is hard breaking old habits. Take it from the old Chuck Rambaldo. I believed that since I was a member of the One True Church, and since I never fell into the traps of those sins such as drugs, alcohol, gambling and infidelity that God was on my side!

In striving to avoid all the pitfalls of life, I was blinded by my own humanness. My sin of pride led me to believe that I had all the answers. Since 1985, I have come to learn that if you allow the spirit to dwell in you, life is a lot easier and more peaceful. The words of the Serenity Prayer are so simple, yet so wise: "God grant me the Serenity to accept those things I cannot change, change the things I can, and the wisdom to know the difference."

That wisdom, I believe, is the indwelling of the Holy Spirit.

My prayer for those of you facing extreme hardships in life is that you awaken to the gifts of the Holy Spirit before you hit the wall. You can survive the battles of life, even from the depths of depression or from other trials and misfortunes; you must simply relinquish the wheel and allow Him to be in control of your life. When there seems to be no hope, no way out, simply surrender. Let go and let God.

My prayer is for those of you raised in the Catholic faith to not give up on God, but to go to the next level of your walk. It's simple; just accept Jesus as your Savior and ask Him into your heart.

When you surrender to Him, He will send the Spirit to live in you. He will never leave you or forsake you. It is then that you will experience what it means to be a new creation in Christ! What a blessing! It's a life choice that will make you complete the sign of the Cross to include The Holy Spirit. And when you read His words,

Take up thy Cross, and follow me daily. Luke 9: 23, you will not only be prepared for life's struggles, but you will be totally equipped to handle them in a serene manner.

Take it from a real Doubting Thomas. I came pushing and shoving, not to get to a better understanding but to run away. It's been more than twenty years since, and I can testify that it works. And each time I make the sign of the Cross, I have a deeper appreciation of who the Holy Spirit is.

Since I first wrote this chapter, I have come to realize that there is a blessing with the infusion of the Holy Spirit, and sometimes there is a curse. As my great friend Jerry Wrobel pointed out to me, "Chuck, read 1 Corinthians 2:10-16."

Now God has revealed them [all things] to us by Spirit, for the Spirit searches everything, even the deep things of God. For who among men knows the concerns of a man except the spirit of God? Now we have not received the spirit of the world, but the Spirit who is from God, in order to know what has been freely given to us by God. We also speak these things, not in words taught by human wisdom, but in those taught by the Spirit, explaining spiritual things to spiritual people. But the natural man does not welcome what comes from God's spirit, because it is foolish to him; he is not able to know it since it is evaluated spiritually. The spiritual person, however, can evaluate everything, yet he himself cannot be evaluated by anyone. For who knows the Lord's mind, that he may instruct Him? But we have the mind of Christ.

What sometimes appears to be a simple decision or a simple matter of agreement can become a disagreement, even a split in the family. It has taken me a long, long time to understand why resolutions do not come easily through long hours of discussions, disagreements, hurts and anger. It is for that simple matter that many of my family, friends and business associates are walking in the natural man's skin, not the Spirit man's.

I continue to pray that those whom I love dearly and are as

hardheaded and unwilling to try to surrender as I was back in 1985 are at least receiving some seed-planting from our life experience together.

The only prayer our Savior said was *Our Father, Who art in heaven, hallowed be thy Name. Thy Kingdom come, Thy will be done, on earth as it is in Heaven. Give us this day our daily bread. And forgive us our trespasses as we forgive those who trespass against us. And lead us not into temptation, but deliver us from evil.* Matthew 6: 9-13.

Now when I make the sign of the Cross, I thank God the Father for creating me, God the Son for dying for my sins on the Cross, and God the Holy Spirit for bringing me back to life.

1963
Learning to be a right handed catcher. Batter Up!

CHAPTER 5

THE WONDER YEARS
1964–1972

For God does not give us a spirit of fear, but a spirit of power, love, and self-discipline. 2 Timothy 1: 7.

Without consultation, plans are frustrated, but with many counselors they succeed. Proverbs 15: 22

I never knew I had God-given baseball talent until I tried out for the seventh grade St. Mary's baseball team. Our coach, Mr. Napoli, was a good mentor in my life although at the time he didn't seem like it. However, he knew something about baseball. When he asked me what position I was strong at, I replied, "Catcher."

He said, "Rambaldo, get your mitt, put on the gear and get behind the plate."

Before the pitcher could even throw a pitch, I heard his voice. "Hold it, hold it, hold it. Rambaldo what are you doing?"

"I'm catching," I answered.

"No, I mean what do you think you're doing, trying to play the position as a left-hander?" Back in those days, there were no left-handed catchers, let alone left-handed catchers' mitts.

He used tact and diplomacy and said, "Since you have a strong desire, go home and teach yourself how to throw right-handed, and next year you'll be our starting catcher." So Dad bought me a right-handed mitt, and all summer and fall I played catch with brother Rick, working on developing my right-handed skills. I couldn't wait for spring to come. When it finally did, I even had my own catcher's mitt. When Mr. Napoli saw me coming, bright-eyed and beaming, he proclaimed, "Rambaldo, let me see if you can throw right-handed." I promptly shot him a rifle bullet with my right hand. I could tell by his expression that he was impressed.

"Get behind home plate," he bellowed. I put on the gear, crouched behind the plate and confidently put the catcher's mask down over my head. Mr. N. told the batter to step in, the pitcher to pitch, and I got ready. The first pitch was a beaut, fast and right down the pike. The batter promptly swung and missed, and so did I. I recall blinking my eyes as the bat, or what seemed to be the bat, came toward my head. I remember the ball hitting the backstop. The sound of a ringing chain link fence is one that you can't miss. Well, even with all my desire and determination, I forgot one of the fundamentals of life: You have to be able to play the position. But as a coach, Mr. Napoli pushed me to do what I didn't think I could. I did make the team and was St. Mary's starting third baseman that year. I got my only letter sweater for it, and I remember until this day how proud I was that my dad attended the banquet.

Another indelible memory of our dad and baseball was when Dad took Rick and me to a Cleveland Indians night game. It went to extra innings and my hero, Tito Francona, hit one right down the right field line where we were seated. From that night on, for any baseball teams I wore number 14, his number, and I also taught myself to bat left-handed for that's what he did. The end result was that I willed myself to be ambidextrous in both hitting and throwing.

St. Mary's was very good to me. There was a certain nun, Sister John Vianney, who was my second grade teacher. Looking back, this was the same time my parents were going through tough times in their marriage, and my grades reflected it. In my mind's eye, I can still see Sister John's smiling face and sense her caring personality. I still have the progress reports where she put on two out of four reports that I was in danger of failing. (See Appendix.)

Those words still haunt me. I didn't want to fail a grade. In my mind,

I felt if that happened, my fears for not only my parents' situation (remember, we were taught that anyone who divorces was not only excommunicated but would be damned to the fires of hell) but also failing a grade would bring more shame on me. I think Sister took a real interest in me because of my home situation and because of her Christian character, or she had discerned what might be going on in my head. It was not all about the studies. She passed me. I say it that way because my Sister John Vianney was most likely my first guardian angel in character development. I got an opportunity to thank her a few years back. She still was as sweet and caring as I recall from my youth.

In recalling my early years, I have to mention my mother's mother, Grandma Lucy. While I'm writing this chapter, she must be looking down and asking What about me? Recently, while I was in DrugMart shopping for soap, I spotted something I had not seen in nearly fifty years, Fels Naptha soap. For years, I have been telling our kids about how Grandma Lucy would wash both Rick's and my faces with it. We would kick and yell, telling her how hard she rubbed and how the soap irritated our skin. Did she listen? No. Now I read on this bar of soap that, not only is Fels Naptha celebrating its 100th anniversary; after all it's the Queen of Clean—but it also cautions "eye and skin irritant" and is ideal for pre-treating stains as a heavy duty laundry bar soap.

In another area of life, Dad taught us to slow down. Please understand, neither of our parents ever sat on the couch at night to relax and watch a little television. They seemed to be always on the go. I think most Italian families back in the '50s and '60s seemed to be like this.

Our family found happiness and enjoyment in multi-tasking. However, Dad seemed to be the one who found the time to take us on vacations. With him we went to Niagara Falls, the hills of Uniontown and Hershey, Pennsylvania, and the Heinz ketchup factory. These weren't planned two-week ordeals, but they were taken enough times that they are pleasant memories for me.

As I became a teenager, things kept looking up. I got my driver's license in '66, got to share ownership of a beautiful black '66 GTO with my brother, and I was going to be the next Gene Krupa or Buddy Rich. I was taking drum lessons at Petromelli's Studio on East 185th Street, right down the road from St. Joe's High School. On my sixteenth birthday, my dad surprised me by taking me for an audition at a fellow worker's home who was a mean drummer. Dad asked him to allow me to demonstrate if "I had it."

After hearing what I was sure was nothing but banging to him, he informed my father that I did, indeed, have "the It factor". Our next stop was a music store. He informed the sales clerk that it was my birthday and that I could pick out a drum set of my liking. I looked around, and made my choice. It was a used set. Dad would have none of that. He bought me a brand new drum set, silver-sparkle, Ludwig-made like Ringo Starr had.

Life couldn't be better. I joined a group called The Flock, played some gigs, got my hair styled, went to all the football and basketball games and dances and cruised the streets with that bad Black Beauty. I was even voted "Joe Viking" (it meant you had spirit) by my classmates and appeared on local TV on *The Jerry G. Show* for my dancing skills, and danced with the prom queen, Nancy Strobel, in my senior year of high school. Don't let anyone tell you those aren't the best years of our lives. But my real dance partner, the best female dancer I ever "cut a rug" with, is Michele. I first met her at a St. Joe's mixer, through her cousin, my classmate, Joey Ganim. I thought she was Italian. She not only looked Italian—she had our rhythm.

Sadly, I must mention that we had to bid the goat (GTO) bye-bye in late '67. The car had been stolen three times in less than ninety days. The insurance company said that was enough! Looking back, the mid-'60s were the greatest times. We had the best music, coolest clothes, toughest muscle cars and most talented local bands and dances! As we all know too well, our high school years come and go in a wink. Then, we try to re-live them the rest of our lives.

When it came time for college, my dad asked me, "Where would you like to go to college?" Brother Rick was attending Ohio University. Our dad was very proud that his two boys would go on to college. I told him I thought John Carroll University was the place for me. He pulled back the window shade in our East Cleveland home and said, "Look outside. Do you realize where we live? John Carroll is for bluebloods." After that, I decided that JCU probably wasn't a realistic choice.

A few weeks later, Dad told me to hop in his station wagon. No mention was made of why or where we were headed. To my surprise, he drove me to the front doors of John Carroll. After I blurted out something about this place being for bluebloods, he told me that if I had the will to attend, he would find the way. I think this may have served as another lesson in character development, and when I was faced with a similar situation with my children, I used my dad's leadership in the matter to guide me.

The next four years were no-nonsense when it came to studying. But, there was always time for music and dancing. Michele and I would sometimes go out four times a week in the summer months. Michele made me look like a rookie when it came to studying. I think there still are two desks in the library with our names on them. We both graduated in the summer of 1972 with our degrees. Michele graduated with honors and even did five years of study in four. My 2.85 GPA with a business degree in management was not bad either.

The fall of '72 brought with it adulthood. It was time to go out into the real world. My first real job was working for Uncle Sam as a second lieutenant in the Army Transportation Corps. I was to be stationed at Ft. Story, Virginia. Now, when I got my orders that read Virginia Beach, I was shocked. All of the other R.O.T.C. grads going to active duty went to Ft. Hood, Texas. Lucky me, though, the guy who couldn't tread water was to be an Amphibious Craft Officer! Ft. Story, you see, sits right on the Atlantic Ocean. Go figure!

1974
Lt. Rambaldo, starched fatigues and all

1984
New Company Car to go
along with our New Custom
Home

1973
Our Wedding Day ~ June 17th, 1973

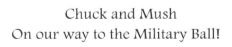

Chuck and Mush
On our way to the Military Ball!

CHAPTER 6

A LIFETIME OF WORLDLY ACCOMPLISHMENTS 1973-1984

What does it profit a man if he gains the whole world, but loses his soul? Mark 8: 36.

The way of a fool is right in his own eyes, but a wise man is he who listens to counsel. Proverbs 12: 15.

There is a current commercial on television that says, "Life comes at you fast". For me it was the decade of my life in my mid-twenties to my mid-thirties that came at me fast. My two years of active duty were equivalent to twenty years of experience in the business world. Not only was I hundreds of miles away from my family and friends, but also this was the first time in my life that the only one I could rely on was me! Initially, it was a hard adjustment. My home away from home as an officer was a shared house off base with another officer, Lt. William Zeir. He also had a liking for music. The one thing that seemed to lift me up when I was down was music. But the problem with Bill was that he played the same song over and over, day in, day out. I still can see and hear the tune as I parked my '69 Charger in the drive. The melody came bellowing out of the windows. "I keep away from Runaround Sue," a classic tune by my favorite recording artist, Dion DiMucci. I wonder if Lt. Zeir has ever gotten over Runaround Sue!

During the time away from Michele, I knew she was the girl for me. I missed her so much. Her genuine and loving ways stood out so much more when I was away and facing the real world. And from the daily phone calls, it was a mutual feeling. Michele took a few trips down to beautiful Virginia, and we discussed our future. I think somewhere between her weekly bowling games, we decided upon a June wedding. She will tell you to this day that I don't cook or clean, but I somehow learned to survive that first year alone in Virginia.

My company commander, Captain Minnich, was a Vietnam vet, a helicopter pilot and airborne paratrooper. When he saw in my military file that I had graduated as a Distinguished Military Graduate (D.M.G.), he gave me the worst platoon and worst platoon sergeant. Ninety-five percent of my men were Vietnam vets who had just returned stateside and had only 60 to 90 days left on active duty. They had been involved with the war, and the last thing they wanted to do was to "play army." I can still hear his welcome speech. He actually put his arm around me and walked me over to the small window in his office. "Look out there. Which platoon do you think I gave you, Lt. Rambaldo?" I pointed to the bunch that was the most unkempt and looked like they didn't want to be there. "Correct, Lt. Rambaldo. What did they teach you in your military training about your platoon sergeant?"

"That he is the backbone of the Army, sir!"

"Great textbook answer, my son. But your Sergeant Cash drinks Listerine. That's how bad an alcoholic he is. I gave you the worst because I think you can make them the best. Formation is 0:600 a.m. If your platoon has to be up and at 'em, bunks made, showered, barracks swept and ready for report by 0:600, what time do you think you might have to show up each morning to assure this?"

"Around 5:45 a.m." was my reply.

"Think again," he said. "Remember, I told you that you have the worst platoon sergeant in the entire battalion. You will most likely have to be on base by 0:400 every morning to not only wake up your men, but you'll have to get your platoon sergeant up also."

Even though as an officer I was afforded the luxury of living off base, for the first year I sleepily turned on my barracks lights every morning around 4:15 a.m. It was not until we found a better home for Sgt. Cash that my life as an officer improved. The one great thing about being exposed to the military is that it is sink or swim. You have to be able to handle, adapt, and cope with a multitude of different individuals from all walks of life while accomplishing your mission and objective, whatever it is. I was awarded lieutenant of the entire post after my first year at Ft. Story, and my Unit 458 did go from the worst to the best! For my reward, I was sent to Puerto Rico for two weeks. I did not go with my wife, however, but with the U.S. Navy and U.S. Marines as part of a joint military operation aboard the USS *Portland*. Can you say seasick and three-minute showers in the same breath? But that's another story!

Another accomplishment I cherish is winning the Physical Combat Proficiency Test in 1972. Mr. Fitness was something I never gave much thought to although my dad did tell us that he ran track with the great Jesse Owens. Just after graduating from college, I was on my way to serve my country, but for three months we had to attend additional officer military training. I was faced with not only trying to perform my best in a military environment, which was new to me, but also to compete with other college grads from various states all over the country. The day that stands out the most was the one where we all took The Test. It consisted of five main events:

Forty-yard crawl
Horizontal Ladder Run
Dodge and Jump
The Grenade Throw
And the Infamous One-Mile Run.

The key accomplishment was to finish first, running a six-minute and twenty-eight second mile in the blistering heat. It had to have been over 90 degrees. I can vividly remember the weight of my combat boots as they hit the asphalt pavement track. We did the test in full military gear. What still is astonishing to me is that I won when competing with individuals who ran track in high school and college and were experienced winners in the field. I never did either.

There is another memory of an individual, who also ran track, but couldn't compete because of a leg injury. Well, he became both my coach and inspiration. He positioned himself strategically where I could see him, and he not only instructed me on how to pace myself, but, in addition, he planted the right positive words that made me want to push on when I had no energy.

The end result was I crossed the finish line FIRST! And not just once, but TWICE, for we had run a preliminary test a few days prior. The guy who came in second vowed that he had never been beaten in track and that after the first time that it would never happen again. When relaying the story to a neighbor, who is a runner, he informed me that I must have given it my all, for I threw up after each marathon.

My score card read 471 out of a possible 500. WOW! God had allowed me to excel in the mile run and to achieve the highest score on the Physical Combat Proficiency Test! (See Appendix.)

The second year of my military life proved hard on married life. Michele and I never seemed to spend much time together, especially holidays and birthdays. I was always out in the field. So, when they asked me to re-up and become what was to be a new position for the military, Race Relations Officer, we chose to return to our home city, Cleveland, Ohio. September 12, 1974, is another day I can see clearly in my mind's eye: Michele and I driving off of Ft. Story, Virginia, for the last time in our green '66 Mustang.

Although we had been married only one year, we already had experienced some of the curves life can throw at you. But little did we know what awaited us back in our hometown. I thought going into the business world would be a snap! After all, I had a business degree from a prestigious university, had served my country for two years as an officer in the U.S. Army and learned how to adjust and mature as a married man while thousands of miles away from home.

You know the saying, Timing is everything? How about looking for a career in a recession? Or your wife landing a job before you do (you Italian men know how hard that is on the old ego!)? What about expecting your first child with no income and no health insurance? And, then your wife being fired because of her pregnancy?

Some welcome home!

When we told my dad that we were going to inform her employer about her pregnancy, Dad's reply was, "Are you out of your minds? They'll fire her in a heartbeat." I told him how out of date he was. It was 1974. There are laws against such things.

When Michele told her boss at the Buick dealership she was pregnant, he replied that the owner said she could work until she wanted to quit. However, it seems that Pop was pretty wise about the ways of this world. That same week, I can still see my pretty young wife, umbrella overhead, tears flowing, as I picked her up after I'd had another unfruitful week of job searching. As she got in the car, she informed me that they had fired her.

After ninety days of pounding the pavement, I took a job as a collector for Household Finance to support my family. In retrospect, it was a good taste of the real world. I started looking for a new position the day I started at Household Finance. After about six months, Michele's family told me that one of their relatives had bought a large manufacturing plant, and that he was looking for someone with my qualifications. My first response was that I didn't think it was a good idea to work for family. Nevertheless, I went through the various interviews and was hired as both the personnel manager and accounting assistant to Frank Dodam at Accurate Die Casting.

I started in March 1975, and quickly found my gift and passion was in dealing with the human resources/labor relations end of the position. When working in this area, my energy level seemed to soar. I was working more than fifty hours a week at Accurate Die Casting, was a first lieutenant in the Army reserves the last weekend of each month, and I enrolled in the first MBA course at John Carroll three nights a week, excluding the long hours spent on homework assignments.

Things seemed to "just come naturally." Married life was great, and we had a beautiful daughter Rochelle in May 1975. We bought our first home in the city where I grew up, Mentor, Ohio, and purchased a brand new 1975 Pontiac Grand Prix. Within two years, we had a baby boy, Chuckie, and bought a new home in Twinsburg. In 1978 I got my MBA and was promoted a few times along the way, eventually to vice president of human resources and labor relations. By this time, Accurate Die Casting had grown from 250 employees, with plants now in Cleveland, Rockford, Illinois, and Fayetteville, New York, to over 1,000 unionized members.

I was a proud papa and had a beautiful wife to impress with my achievements. She was the best mom anyone could ever be, and our children were her delight. When it came to family gatherings, everyone gathered at our house. Michele loves cooking; her dad was in the restaurant business for over forty years. Both of our families love her hospitality and very tasty meals. We were starting to enjoy the fruits of my hard work and long hours. Michele didn't have to work and could be at home with the kids. Reflecting on it, I wanted a family life to come home to and envisioned for our kids the perfect family life that I never knew.

With my vice presidency came much more of a salary, fringe benefits and a company car, along with more traveling and demands on my time. It seemed I was forever boarding a plane. Having had a father who was a blue-collar worker and union steward helped my understanding of unions and the blue-collar mentality. I learned and was brought up on the fact that no matter what your education, life style, or ethnic background, everyone wants the truth and can sense if you're giving them "a con job." To be a man of your word at times may be the hard road to choose, but when dealing with people, it's the only path to go down. We had been so successful in developing an atmosphere throughout our facilities of striving to bring out the best in people, production, safety, and quality that we were featured in *Blue Book Magazine* in 1979. (See Appendix.) Accurate was considered one of the best mid-sized unionized manufacturing companies in America to learn from. "Every employee a manager" was our motto. In 1980, Accurate acquired another die casting firm with a long rich history—Milwaukee Die Casting. All of our plants had such a history. The Fayetteville, New York, plant was the oldest, starting in 1903. This plant was also unionized, and now I was chief negotiator for four unionized facilities. All had different contracts and expiration dates. In a ten-year span, I was chief negotiator on twelve different contractual agreements. You guessed it. I was like Ricky Nelson, "A Traveling Man."

Looking back, it's easy to see that it was during this time that "The Rust Bucket," the decline of manufacturing firms in America, was taking place. From 1980 until 1985 I was either negotiating a contract or re-negotiating for wage freezes or concessions. The positive environment we had worked hard to create through organizational development took a back seat to survival.

Now, it was time to listen to the music! Even though The Flock never broke out of Cleveland, my therapy for years was playing my drums to 45s in the rec room of our home. I had made it a practice of stopping at the world famous Tommy Edwards Records to pick up my favorite tunes. In 1981, the store's founder died suddenly. I asked the right questions about its future, and soon Rick and I were putting in a sealed bid to purchase it. Mom wanted to work again, and Michele was looking for a part-time job since the kids were now in school.

Did you ever have everything in life seem to be going your way so that you had to pinch yourself to see if it was real? Here I was, at just thirty-two, a vice president of a major manufacturing firm, a co-owner of a well established Cleveland record store, I was driving a new company car, a triple blue '98 Olds, as well as owning a '75 black custom Corvette, a rare Opel GT and a new Dodge Charger for Michele. I had a loving wife, with two beautiful children now attending a Catholic school. When they asked me what we were going to do next, I exclaimed, "We're going to Disneyworld!"

Once again, in 1983, I was packing my bags and negotiating in Fayetteville and Milwaukee. I was re-negotiating with the UAW in New York, the plant that should have been the most productive and profitable. It was the largest and most modern, yet the attitude of labor was constant distrust. We were forced to replace the workers in a bitter strike in 1982, and the result was a one-year agreement. That's why I was back up there in '83. It was during the summer that I learned Dad had cancer.

From June 1 until mid-November was a tough period for all of our family. When I was not out of town, I would either travel to Dad's home and bring him chocolate almond, his favorite ice cream, or take him for a chemotherapy treatment or visit him in the hospital. It was not our first experience with the disease. We had lost Michele's Aunt Eve and a sister-in-law, Sherry, a few years earlier. But when it's a member of the family that has been with you since day one, it's a lot harder. We were blessed to have a great family friend, Mary DiDonato, who was a skilled nurse. She was the individual who took charge and made sure that Dad had the best doctors and skilled care. She arranged for Dad to be in a place where he was comfortable, his home. He had round-the-clock care. Such care had a new name, hospice, a new type of treatment for the terminally ill.

In between my out-of-town trips, I was at my father's home trying to aid and give him some comfort like he had provided me over the years. It was during this time that the Twinsburg charismatic prayer group offered to visit and pray with Dad. When I asked him if he felt comfortable with this, he simply nodded his head. When Jerry and Grace Wrobel, who headed the group, prayed the sinner's prayer with him and asked him if he accepted Jesus as his Savior, he nodded his head again. Although I was very leery of their practices, the prayer group seemed to minister on a level that worked. Please remember, I was still a doubting Thomas at this time. But these Pentecostal Catholics appeared to have an approach that delivered an inner peace that was hard to find elsewhere.

When Michele and I heard the phone ring at 4:44 a.m. that cold November 13, I knew that Dad had passed on. The great gift that God gave me at that time was that I had no regrets. There was no If onlys… If only I had done this with him… If only I had never said those words… If only I had been more involved with his life or he with mine. There was none of that. There was nothing to If only about. It's now been more than twenty years, and I miss him and think of him often. I am so grateful that when it came to my life, he was a man of his word. Because of that, I feel the sixty-four years of his life and the thirty-three of those I was fortunate to spend with him were a blessing to me and to all those whose lives he touched.

It's odd, though we nicknamed him Grumpie, that is not the way we remember him. His spirit leaves you with gratitude that he was a part of your life, and his words endure in my heart these many years after his passing. Till this day, many family members or friends of the family recount experiences with our dad and how he touched their lives in a warm and positive manner.

When God takes something or someone away from you, he replaces it with something or someone else for your good. The key is remembering: it's all in His time! In my case, He has allowed my mom to become that someone to replace my dad. She and I have become very close since my father died. The purchase of the store was supposed to allow her to once again do some of the things she loves to do—be in and around music, the public, and rub elbows with some of the recording artists. These years have allowed me to get to know her better and appreciate her business talents as well as her motherly love.

Anyone who has ever owned and operated a family business knows that there can be trying times and situations. Many times such experiences can tear a family apart. Yet, it is my father's words that linger whenever I think about that warm summer "father-to-son talk" on the stoop in Mentor. He was right. Choices in life are sometimes hard, but you have to be a man of your word. "A man isn't a man if he can't be trusted, and trust begins with your word," he exclaimed. This was the rule of thumb that guided my every decision, whether consciously or sub-consciously. Sure, my folks were divorced. I may have not learned much by their example in the how-to's in raising a family under one roof. But I had learned a lesson from my father's words that would make me good at anything I tried to do—husband, father or a businessman.

In the middle of 1984, I decided our little hometown of Twinsburg was being ruined by development and chain stores. When the Golden Arches sign went up and lit up our bedroom window, the For Sale sign went up in our yard. We found a great custom homebuilder on the west side close to our retail business and close to Mom. So Michele was soon at her best designing the home of our dreams. Like every American, we thought building your own custom home meant you'd made it! I always said that at age thirty-five I would retire. I somehow knew working at that pace and with that degree of stress couldn't go on forever. Even though my passion for family, fun and a great work ethic had carried me to a degree of success I never had dreamed of, little did I know that within thirty days of moving into our dream home, my desire to succeed and to be a man of my word would be challenged!

I had no foresight to see the darkness that lay immediately ahead. I had originally planned on titling this book *On Top at Thirty-Five and the Next Day Hardly Alive*! Is anyone ever prepared for a journey through hell? Maybe not, but listening to those who have traveled such a road might help you to survive such an experience a little more easily than I did.

I hope by reading my life's experience to date was entertaining. Now, strap on your seatbelts and get ready for the true grit portion. For you see, I thought by being a man of my word, relying upon my physical and mental abilities and assuring my deeds were always in line with God's teachings, I was protected from the evils of this world.

For thirty-five years, I had successfully run on the teachings of the family, the church, strong educational systems and the business world, but I was unknowingly embryonic in my spiritual walk. This doubting Thomas saw the light only when the headlights shown brightly after the train wreck.

1980's
The three Human Resources Mgrs.
Duane, Wayne, Jimmy and Chuck

CHAPTER 7

1985: CLINICALLY DEPRESSED

He reveals mysteries from the darkness and brings the deep darkness into light. Job. 12: 22.

But the night continues and I am continually tossing until dawn. Job 7: 4.

So that my soul would choose suffocation Death rather than my pain, I wasted away; I will not live forever. Leave me alone for my days are but a breath. Job 7: 15-16.

We all have an inner sense of what is right and what is wrong. We all think we know what we are doing when we are doing it. But isn't it funny how clear things become once we have had time to reflect and look back upon previous decisions in life?

It's been almost twenty-five years since 1985, and it's clear to me that I did have an inner sense of what was right during my journey along the bumpy roads of industry. But I thought I knew best because what I had relied upon to get me through the trials had worked so well for me and mine until then. Sometimes things seem to go from bad to worse. That surely was the case during the summer of 1985. The beginning of 1985 saw my time involved with asking for wage freezes in Milwaukee and Fayetteville. We had already made the hard choice to close our Rockford, Illinois facilities. That left Cleveland—the plant where it all began.

There were the middle-of-the-night phone calls to my motel room, threatening my life and that of the late H. Wayne Panciera, who worked with me in Fayetteville as the human resources manager. There were the plane trips to all of our locations to meet with union officials to seek mutually workable ways to assure that Accurate remained in business. Even in a depressed economy, our employees were a productive bunch. This was especially true in Cleveland; these employees worked with the oldest equipment but had the best knowledge, work ethic and dedication to get the job done.

The owner's plan of action for Cleveland was to move the facilities to a more modern plant in Medina. He gave me my marching orders in the fall of 1984 to obtain a ninety-day extension of the current labor agreement to afford him more time to obtain the required financing for such a move. When ninety days came and went, he requested that I seek an additional ninety days. Both requests were achieved.

Lo and behold, just as the second ninety-day period was coming to an end, the owner told me that the company needed a third ninety days. The economy was to blame, he said, and the bankers were dragging their feet on the necessary funding.

God's gift to me was to be able to discuss and mutually satisfy the major concerns with all parties involved while developing a history of trust, belief and results. The company had relied on me for nearly a decade to be the go-to guy in times of need. Because I had developed a credibility factor throughout the firm with both the U.A.W. and the I.A.M., there were many times the union employees chose to hang in there with us and ride out the storm. This was largely due to the reputation of credibility and trust our organization had achieved over the years. No one could ever say that I tried to pull the wool over their eyes about the true picture that Accurate Die Casting was facing.

It was at this time that I decided to talk with the owner alone. I was beginning to have my doubts. My other mentor, Mac Horton, had always advised me that business relationships were like bank accounts. Some days they are very positive, and some days they are negative. But a bank will not close your account for a few bouncers. He thought it best not to do so with people in our lives. But when that relationship remains negative more than it is positive, it's time to close the relationship. To that point, the owner's account in my life had remained positive.

I asked the owner to lay it on the line and be up front about our circumstances. I walked into his corporate office where the colored photo hung of him kissing the Pope's ring along with photos of his entire family. Immediately, he took control of the meeting by starting with three dramatic things:

He threw out multiple colored pills from his pockets, and explained that these were medicine for his heart (he had suffered a heart attack a few years back) and that if we did not obtain this extension, the company would eventually close, and his wife and five children would lose everything.

The owner informed me that he had fired his own brother, along with the vice president of engineering. I had always said they were dismantling our company.

Then, he took keys from his other pocket and threw them down, along with blueprints, on his desk. He informed me that I should arrange to take the business agent, along with the union committee, to see the new facilities in Medina.

Now, I ask you, is there any reason not to believe the guy?

He was the one who had worked, negotiated and made success happen over the past ten years, taking Accurate from a little more than two hundred employees to nearly two thousand. He built it from a twelve-million dollar concern to one that shipped over fifty million dollars a year.

Please remember, I was raised to be a man of my word. I knew how to sell an agreement if it truly was for the betterment of the company. I had successfully done so for a decade. I had negotiated over ten labor agreements with four different unions in four different states. But hidden agendas were a first for me.

So I put on my best suit and held another meeting with the union, this time down at union headquarters. Not only were the business agent and union committee present but the head of the local sat in.

After I explained our request and the reasons for it, the top man spoke up. "You know I have been hearing this same stuff for the past couple of years—Warner Swayze, Addressograph, Multigraph, and so on." He was naming locally owned Cleveland institutions that had requested that the union work with management and then closed the doors. "You guys aren't planning on closing the doors, are you?"

A definite NO was my response. Still they were concerned. The workers confided in me. Even though they trusted me, they smelled something very fishy in the management of other areas of the company. They well understood that cash was tight. But why wasn't Accurate paying some medical bills? Accurate had chosen to try to save money a few years back and self-insured its employees' health plans.

Even after viewing the future site of Accurate in Medina, the committee was not unified in granting a ninety-day extension. The business agent pushed the extension claiming, "Chuck, we are granting this third request because of you. You have never led us wrong. You have been a tough but fair negotiator. We do not trust Slyman, but because of you, we will grant him a third extension."

I, too, had some inner doubts about the current situation, but now, hopefully, we had obtained the needed time to get the job done. Wrong! One of the first things the owner did after the extension was to drive in with a new red Mercedes convertible. Then, he announced he was taking his family to Italy for a vacation.

As the days wore on and the bills piled up, I was constantly approached by various employees (union and management) as to why vacation pay wasn't being paid, hospital bills were past due and normal operating expenses were going unpaid. I approached the vice president of finance about these developing conditions and also inquired what our financial package was going to be for the union negotiations.

As I was asking the VP these questions, he got up and closed the door to his office. His comments still ring in my mind as I mentioned earlier. "Do you know that new company car you're driving, that nice salary and fringe benefits of yours? We will all have them in ten years down the road, but those poor bastards out in the shop, they're f….. This plant will be a ghost town in ninety days."

Ninety days! I walked out of his office numb. I was numb for weeks. I was probably in shock and disbelief. I wanted to hear it from the owner. I needed to know that this was not the end. I may have pictured the end if we all tried our best and failed and the company closed. But deceit and betrayal had never entered my mind.

If you haven't seen that famous final courtroom scene in the movie, *And Justice for All*, rent it or buy it! Al Pacino, the lead character, is forced to choose between the security of his prestigious career and his personal integrity. Imagine that! Pacino, playing a trial lawyer defending a prominent judge, finds out that his Mr. Clean-client is guilty of rape. He wrestles with the shame that his client chose—"winning" regardless of the truth, regardless of justice, regardless of the law! During his opening remarks, Pacino chooses to tell the truth: that his client is, indeed, GUILTY, and it cost Pacino dearly. This was a similar journey that I unknowingly was to embark upon. I was trapped.

I experienced a nervous breakdown and was most likely clinically depressed while I tried to hang on working until the owner returned from Europe. I can't tell you the anguish, the disbelief, and the searching for an alternative that went on and on in my head. When I went home and shared this horror story with my wife, she cried. She couldn't believe it. We agreed that if this was what was being planned, and I was the lamb being sent to slaughter, our only choice was the right one—the hard one—to resign. But, even with coming to that conclusion, I still hoped for a positive solution. I wrestled with disbelief that a man could make such a choice and knowingly put someone in an inescapable position. I am afraid his choice is one I will carry to my grave.

In retrospect, many times I found myself second guessing myself as to why I didn't see this happening. Why didn't I leave the scene before the crash? Why did I try to fix the unfixable? Could it have been in God's divine plan? Might it have been this was a part of my divine assignment? My blessing, and sometimes my curse, is the wisdom of knowing and doing what is right. God bestowed this upon me at an early age. Maybe I stood it for too long because I simply had to; it was not only a part of my character, but it was a part of His plan. Some plan! Pictures of employees and their families seem to run across the landscape of my mind: the births of their children, anniversaries, 25-year award banquets, baseball teams, visions of the employees working hard on the factory floor day after day, year after year. I now knew something that was about to shatter their lives. I now knew I was a part of it. I began to wake up during the night. I cried and trembled in the shower. I could not eat. Then I reflected upon my own family. How could I have led them into this trap? In retrospect, my priorities of life were totally out of line. They were:

The World's Priorities		God's Priorities
Fortune (money)		God
Fame, acceptance, being known	vs.	Family
		Job
Power		
Pleasure		

If I resigned, where would our income come from? We were fortunate enough to have Michele home with our children. Mine was the only income. Unknowingly, I was clinically depressed. That condition to this day isn't real. I had never taken any kind of medicine for any similar symptoms.

Well, after what seemed an eternity, I resigned. Having been raised to do the right thing, tell the truth, be a man of my word, the position I was put into was a choice without a choice. You think you know what it is to go through tough times, until God allows you to be in some waters that are way over your head, and the undertow is devastating.

I would like to share an opinion from someone who was deeply involved with the work I was doing in our Fayetteville plant, the late H. Wayne Panciera:

Chuck Rambaldo interviewed me, hired me, and I reported to him as the Human Resource Manager in 1979, after I retired with 22 years of active Air Force service. Chuck and I did a lot of labor relations work together. In spite of the union's bad feelings towards the owner, they always respected and liked Chuck; he had a wonderful sense of humor and ready smile, and rarely, if ever, showed anger.

The last contract negotiation in which I was involved occurred in 1983. We asked the union for concessions, the union refused, and a strike ensued. The company advertised for replacement workers. Chuck and I, working out of his motel room, hired workers to cross the picket line. This ordeal was the most stressful situation I was ever involved in. I left the company in 1985. It was not long after that the owner filed for bankruptcy, and shortly thereafter the whole corporation dissolved. Chuck and I have kept in touch over the years. I was really saddened at what happened to him and his family.

During all these years I can't think of anyone more loyal and dedicated to the company than Chuck. He devoted whatever time and effort was required to do his job and support the company much of the time away from his family. Everyone with Accurate Die Casting shared in this unfortunate experience. Many, sadly, lost not only their jobs but also their retirement. Chuck Rambaldo put his heart and soul into his job, and I'm sure he felt betrayed. I might add that the worst thing that happened to me was when I found out how it affected Chuck and his family. We spoke on the phone many times, and I knew how badly he was hurting. All the negative events have positive reactions. Chuck overcame this sad event and is a better man physically and spiritually. He is a great example for those who have felt despair.

Another individual, Patty Scragg-Hudec, who worked closely with me at Accurate Die Casting, shared her experiences during this time:

Jim Siggers, Personnel Manager, and Chuck Rambaldo, V.P. Human Resources and Labor Relations, interviewed and hired me in February of 1979. Chuck was always flying to our various plants to work mostly on union matters. He had one of the most high-pressured positions at the company but always did it with grace and ease.

When I started with the firm, things were upbeat and growing. Around late 1980 and 1981, things started to change. The owner had brought in some new officers that were, in my opinion, not respected by the majority of the employees. Because he was highly involved with labor contracts in our other plant locations, I saw less and less of Chuck, and each time that I did see him, he wasn't himself. Chuck resigned in the summer of 1985, and by September of that year the company filed for bankruptcy.

It was a mess. Vacation pay was never paid, there were no severance packages and, worst of all, no pensions. To this day, I can't figure out how a company that was so successful and respected within its field went by the wayside in such a short period of time.

Michele, Rochelle, Chuckie and I struggled through each summer day until September 3, 1985. I fought to get through every day, and each one was an eternity. I know you have heard people tell how hard it was to get through a day, thus the slogan One Day at a Time. It got so bad that I prayed to make it through one hour. Someone once told me that depression is S L O W wisdom. Very accurate!

Another teaching I recently heard on WCLV radio was that each of us has a Divine Assignment. That each of us brings a piece of God's character to the table of life. My mind kept going backwards: If only I had…He couldn't have…Why did this happen to me and my family? How can we ever get out of this? There was no purpose to getting up each morning, and I had no energy… I tried to stay in bed as long as possible.

Finally, on September 3, 1985, I agreed to be admitted to the hospital. But another fear set in. How were we ever going to pay for it? We had no income, no insurance. Being admitted to St. Luke's hospital's psych ward is a day that is very vivid to me. All kinds of thoughts ran through my head. Are they going to give me shock treatments? Will I ever get out of here? How can I ever work in my career field again after this? All I can tell you is that God is merciful. My stay was less then two weeks. The low point was having to put together a wooden fish with a class of my peers. And the high points were visits from my wife and children. My psychiatrist's analysis was that I was simply "on strike." Anyone who accomplished so much in so little a time desired a rest. Some resting place!

After I was released, I had renewed energy and a desire to try to resume my career path. After seven interviews with a firm called RB&W, I was hired with a similar title and more money. I was back, or so I thought. In just a few hours at my new desk, I realized that I was not going to be able to do this. My new supervisor had me reading minutes of various meetings with the different plants and unions, and it was like reading the horrific ending of Accurate Die Casting. After much anguish, one week after I started, I resigned.

What kind of God has someone fall so deep, picks them up, and then just when all seems well, everything goes to hell again?

From October 1985 until May 1986, I wrestled with Does this surrendering your life to Jesus Christ really work? Just when you think, Yeah, I made the greatest decision in my life in letting go and letting God...! One Day at a Time...Sweet Surrender... Turning my life over to Jesus...willfully surrendering my life to a higher power...Believing I can do all things through Jesus Christ who strengthens me. I tried to hold onto these thoughts. I read my Bible daily even though it was difficult to concentrate because the horror of the situation I had placed my family in kept creeping in. Although I was working on keeping our family together as a unit, things kept going from bad to worse.

After resigning from RB&W, things went into a tailspin again. That little voice kept saying, "See, what are you trying for? You and your Savior can never get you out of this one. What kind of promises are those Christians selling you? You turned your life over and it ain't working, is it? Admit it!"

Without the prospect of a job, I was really fearful again. So, I re-directed my mission on trying to re-group and preserve our family unit. That's where loving individuals and family members begin to question, judge and revert to what their family values are. And of course, in a marriage both families have different perspectives of reality. Things got so bad that Michele and I separated, divorce papers were filed, and outside sources were pulling us in different directions. Now, I began to get really angry with God once again. What kind of God would allow a serving servant to lose it all— materially, financially, and emotionally? Now, he was allowing my last hope, my family, to crumble before my eyes.

For whatever reason, God placed a professional named Terry Drake in my path during this period. He was a real life savior. He allowed me to visit him in the Southwest General Hospital psych unit at no charge. It was a place to hang out when there was no place to go. I remember what an effort it was just to get presentable. What used to take me a half hour to get cleaned up and dressed took triple the time, and I still looked terrible. Why is it when you're feeling rotten on the inside, you look it on the outside? Well, when you have nothing to look forward to, the only thing you look forward to is sleep—and once again, that evades you.

What an illness. Not only does depression zap you of all energy, it carries a stigma. People understand bankruptcy, divorce, deadbeat daddies and moms, broken bones, but not broken brains and hearts.

Another group that God put in my path was EA—Emotions Anonymous. A Christian friend, Marcia Ostrowski, called me. She knew of my walk in the valley and was well aware that I was getting tired of trying this and trying that. But when I attended my first EA meeting in a Brecksville church, I knew this was something genuine and good. I kept going back. Don't get the idea things were getting better; there were just things happening in my life that gave me the spark to try to see what tomorrow might bring. In addition to losing my career, my worldly possessions, my mind, my family, now the retail store our family operated and owned was going down the tubes. We put that up for sale also. There was nothing, nothing that said, "Ain't you glad you're born again?"

As my depression reappeared, I fought those unthinkable, non-Christian, insane thoughts: *It's time to end it all. You gave it that valiant Rambaldo fight, but now face it, admit it. It's over. Even if you survive this, you'll be a disgrace to your family. How about making it look like it's an accident? It's winter. You could take the car, drive into a big old tree, and your family would at least have your insurance money and good memories.* And there were thoughts of just going into the garage and turning on the Corvette and going to sleep. Or how about sticking your head in a gas stove?

Believe it or not, I made a choice. One morning, I got in the 1982 Dodge Charger and drove back to Twinsburg. You see, there was a huge oak tree at the bend in the road. Well, how perfect. It was a snowy, ice-covered road. I lost control as I tried to navigate the curve. BAM! So, do you think I gave it a whirl? I must have sped up upon that scene at least a dozen times that morning. And every time, that little voice in my head said, "What if? What are you doing? What the hell is the matter with you? What if you don't die and only get paralyzed?" So, every time, I pulled the wheel away from crashing into that big oak.

I have never told this part of my journey to anyone in my family. At the time this was for fear of being committed, and up until now, what good would it have done?

Thank God, I still had some family support. Every weekend my brother Rick would drive all the way in from his home in Rochester, New York, just to be with me. In addition, I still can see my mom praying at the foot of my bed as I was cursing and hitting walls.

But nothing seemed to be working: the anti-depressants my psychiatrist had me on, the daily visits to Terry Drake, the weekly visits to EA, the reading of self-help books, the praying, reading His Word, the prayer group's prayers.

When Jerry Wrobel sat at our kitchen table in North Royalton, Ohio, and asked me if I wished to surrender my life to Jesus Christ, and I answered, desperately, "YES." I expected a miracle. I wanted a miracle. I needed a miracle.

I was about to give up when I thought this heaviness, this loneliness, this energy-lessness, this being trapped in my mind, this eternity in hell would never end. Just when I questioned for the umpteenth time, "Born again?" Sure. He'll take, he'll carry, he'll give you the peace the world can't offer you.

One night I went to bed on my Uncle Arnold's birthday, May

7, 1986—broken, depressed, helpless and hopeless—but still believing, I think.

I awoke May 8 with a new feeling. That heaviness had been lifted. Those dark, dreary thoughts erased. There was an inner peace I can't explain, but somehow I knew I was a changed man. That Spirit that all those Born-agains had told me about was somehow a part of me. Please remember, nothing had changed on my outside world. It was still crumbling. But inside was a new person. Could it have been that New Creation in Christ that my Christian leaders had been telling me about?

1983
Work, Work, Work – But in which direction was I headed?

CHAPTER 8

SOMETIMES YOU GOTTA GO TO HELL IF YOU WANNA GET TO HEAVEN

Dear friends, do not be surprised at the painful trial you are suffering, as though something strange were happening to you. But rejoice that you participate in the sufferings of Christ, so that you may be overjoyed when His glory is revealed. 1 Peter 4: 12-13.

But this one thing I do forgetting those things which are behind, and reaching forth unto those things which are before. Philemon 13: 14.

Truly, truly, I say unto you unless one is born again he cannot see the kingdom of God. John 3: 3.

Well, if you know anything about doing a change of face, St. Paul on the road to Damascus is the leader of the pack. He was going out and slaying the Christians as a great Jewish soldier, and one day a bolt of lightning struck him, blinded him for awhile and he saw the light. He is my favorite saint. How can a guy think he's so right one moment and totally change in an instant? Could it be God warned him a few times, then popped him to get his attention? Whatever it was, his words constantly inspire me.

When Michele and I were dancing fools back in high school, one of our favorites tunes was "I Just Want to Testify" (what your love has done for me) by the Parliaments. That's exactly how I felt once He lifted that darkness and heaviness around me on the night of May 7. Remember, I went from being a doubting Thomas to a Testifying One. Anybody listening?

What credibility did I have in that time period? What is the probability of your listening to advice from someone who recently went bankrupt in their business? Or listening to the demons-of-rum speech from an alcoholic? At least, so they appear to the winners of this world!

In my religious beliefs, we aren't raised to praise, share, and shout for joy. We are to be more "doers by example." Thus, we tend to pray silently to ourselves, and in church pray quietly as a group.

Now the New and Improved Chuck Rambaldo was ready to share with those who would listen how great God's love is if you choose to accept His grace and surrender your life. All the while I was remembering that such surrender and inner peace and contentment arrives in His time. Even though I knew that it would take me some time to get through the muck on issues I had to deal with, face and work through, I knew that on May 8, 1986, something wonderful had occurred in my life, and it was not man-made.

Kindly remember, I had been stumbling around for nearly one full year, and nothing seemed to work or improve my state of mind. When I went to see the psychiatrist and informed him that I was cured and I no longer required his antidepressants, he allowed me to get off them slowly.

On my last visit with him, I asked him his professional opinion as to what he thought cured me. This doctor was the head of the psychiatric unit at the hospital and was respected and renowned in his field.

His reply stays with me until this day. "I don't know what got you this way, and even worse, I don't know how you got better."

I knew.

In the words of St. Paul, *If anyone is in Christ, he is a new creation; old things have passed away; behold, all things have become new.* 2 Corinthians 5: 17

Now comes the reprogramming part. As Catholics, we were taught that you can work your way into heaven and that you can pray your loved ones out of purgatory.

Do you know what the Holy Spirit first opened my eyes to see? Those teachings were wrong.

Just as I once failed to see, my family and many of my friends don't have a clear understanding that there is a difference between religion and Christianity. Religion operates on the basis of works: Follow a certain ritual, complete a certain list of required things, and you have arrived. Christianity says that NOTHING you can do earns you favor with God. *Not by works of righteousness which we have done, but according to His mercy He saved us.* Titus 3:5-7. Works do not add up to salvation.

The most challenging person to lead to Christ, in my experience, is the "good person". Such a person believes "I haven't done anything wrong so I don't need forgiveness. I do good things and God will reward me." Such a person believes in his or her heart of hearts that God is motivated by our good works to save us. I was such a believer.

With goodness, pride can creep in ever so gently. I can reflect upon how hard I worked to avoid the pitfalls of this earth, staying away from certain things that could harm my body (cigarettes, alcohol, and drugs). I never smoked a cigarette or consumed any amounts of liquor or even tried an illegal drug. I strived to be a good husband and father, didn't commit adultery and took time not only to support my family but also to be a part of their daily lives. The list went on and on: Don't cheat or practice deceit, attend Mass every Sunday, be good to others. I mastered that list and, take it from me, it's a hard list to master.

I figured if I worked hard on not doing that which offended my God and worked on doing good, I would be protected by the Big Guy. And for thirty-five years the system worked perfectly. Please remember, my belief was based upon performing good works and deeds. Thus, I was one of the most challenging persons to be led to Christ!

As I have traveled my journey these past twenty-five years, it has slowly become more evident that many of my friends and family possess similar religious beliefs as I did. In addition, it also has become apparent that I have a passion in my heart to at least offer what He has done for me to the old Chuck Rambaldos of this world. I remind everyone that I did not choose this path. God had renewed my Spirit. Now I had to re-evaluate my beliefs and focus on the renewing of my mind. I found myself with a new thirst to read the Bible. Now empowered by the Holy Spirit, I had a new ability to understand it.

Again Paul tells us, *Do not be conformed to this world, but be transformed by the renewing of your mind.* Romans 12: 2.

Jerry and Grace Wrobel kept instructing me to get into The Word—to try to understand and answer the question Are you IN this world or are you OF it? Try to focus on that which is above, not that which is below.

For someone who was embryonic in my walk, these were monumental tasks and questions to answer. You probably have heard the saying, "What you need to do is cut some Scripture". One of the things I tried to do daily was read the Bible. One Scripture passage that Michele led me to was Ephesians 6: 10-19:

Last of all I want to remind you that your strength must come from the Lord's mighty power within you. Put on all of God's armor so that you will be able to stand safe against all strategies and tricks of Satan. For we are not fighting against people made of flesh and blood, but against persons without bodies, the evil rulers of the unseen world, those mighty satanic beings and great evil princes of darkness who rule this world; and against huge numbers of wicked spirits in the spirit world. So use every piece of God's armor to resist the enemy whenever he attacks, and when it is all over, you will still be standing up. But to do this, you will need the strong belt of truth and the breastplate of God's approval. Wear shoes that are able to speed you on as you preach the Good News of peace with God. In every battle you will need faith as your shield to stop the fiery arrows aimed at you by Satan. And you will need the helmet of salvation and the sword of the Spirit, which is the Word of God.

Pray in the Spirit all the time. Plead with him, reminding him of your needs, and keep praying earnestly for all Christians everywhere. Pray for me, too, and ask God to give me the right words as I boldly tell others about the Lord, and I explain to them that his salvation is for Gentiles too.

Here lies the key to my rebirth. Please re-read Ephesians 6: 10-19. Initially, as I read this I wondered what exactly He was talking about. We battle NOT against flesh and blood. Pray in the spirit all the time. Strength comes from the Lord's mighty power within you…and especially His salvation is for the Gentiles, too. I believe, some two decades since my depression, that most of us are offered the opportunity to advance to a higher level of protection from the evils of this world by choosing to tap into what Ephesians teaches us. Most people, like me, simply believe that we have the answers. Since we were instructed in school on how to lead a good life and be a good person, our goodness will protect us from the evils of this world. Nothing is farther from the truth.

My daughter Rochelle and I recently had lunch with Ernie Sobieski, my friend, classmate, and attorney. After we visited our alma mater, John Carroll University, he shared with us over lunch that our education was a good one, in fact, a great one, but one area it failed to inform, prepare and teach us about was evil.

That's what I believe was the key element to my nearsightedness. I was never prepared to take on the evil forces of this world. Prepared? I never knew whom I was truly fighting. After years of studying His Word, I can tell you it not only unlocks the truths of this world, it opens your eyes to see, think, and react clearly. My cousin, Joe Comai, and I were talking about a recent sermon I had heard from a Catholic priest. I said to Joe that this priest urged us to pray for our deceased loved ones. "You never know when your prayers send a lost loved one from purgatory into heaven." When I heard that, I shook my head in disbelief and nudged my wife as if to say, Do you hear what he's saying? It's 2005, not 1965.

As I was telling this to Joe, who is 55, he replied, "I applaud that priest."

Even after I challenged him with "What about the shed blood of Jesus Christ? The Passion? The Cross? The Crucifixion? What was all that about, Joe, if not to offer us sinners salvation?"

"Chuck," he said in a relaxed voice, "did you forget, Jesus died on the cross to open the gates of heaven?"

Shocking! He still believes that the entire essence of our faith is that Jesus just opened the gates so we can work our way in! Please understand, I don't profess to have all the answers. Mine is just one witness. Mine is from someone who thought he had the right answers. Mine is to offer hope to the hopeless. Mine is to reach out to someone who may have been trained like me or thinks like I did. Mine is to plant a seed.

But I can tell you that in my experience, sometimes you do have to go to hell in order to get to heaven. I traveled that train. I think that God does allow us trials and tribulations in order to see him more clearly. And in my case, when I felt as if every day, hour, minute, second of my year in hell was too much to bear, He taught me differently. And once He lifts that weight from you, you know what a gift His grace is and what a blessing The Holy Spirit is in your life. It's twenty years later, and I feel more confident every day in my belief. As we used to say at EA, "It works, if you work it!"

I think that there are many suffering Christians that need to understand that there is a way out and that working your way out of hell could get you into heaven. But as with most tests, you must be willing to do the work, make the right choices, and follow His guidance. It all boils down to having faith. Faith that you may not understand the journey you're on, but you know He will get you through it.

Another facet of my religious upbringing was what we call "Catholic guilt". As a good person, you are susceptible to a "left hook" when that inner spirit informs you that something "ain't right in Denmark" about a certain person, and you voice it. Then one of those individuals either in your family, social circle or church chimes in and reminds you, "Wait a minute, did you forget your teachings?" Turn the other cheek. Judge not yet ye be judged. You call yourself a Christian and this is how you act? You must forgive like Jesus did, seventy times seven! After wrestling with many business, personal, and family relationships, I can tell you from my experience that there is a fine line between Christian and victim. C.S. Lewis says "grace abuse" stems from a confusion of condoning and forgiving. "To condone an evil is simply to ignore it, to treat it as if it were good. But forgiveness needs to be accepted as well as offered if it is to be complete: and a man who admits no guilt can accept no forgiveness."

The Word of God was written for our instruction, to teach and train us, we're told in 2 Timothy 3:16. Written on the pages of The Bible are truths of life, health and peace. If we fall, we can stand again. By embracing these truths, we are healed if sickness comes. As we mature through prayer and the Word, our inner man doesn't have to fall prey to deception. We can effectively stand, prevail and conquer when an attack comes. Philip Yancey quotes C.S. Lewis's words, "Embrace the Word of God as your safeguard."

At this time I was hungry to try to figure out how I ever got this way. The one thing I knew was that part of my thought process was flawed. It became apparent that I needed to do soul searching, and a refreshing part of that was re-programming my inner spirit. My re-building project was many-faceted. I continued to attend EA meetings. I tuned into daily radio programs by the Minirth-Meir Clinic. Michele and I continued meeting with Terry Drake and attending a weekly Bible study class for nearly eight years. I started reading a lot of self-help, Christian-based books. One book that opened my eyes wider was *How to Survive an Attack* by Roberts Liardon. In it, he said some things I had never thought of or was trained to think about. The essence of his message is that we fight evil daily, and most of us are not properly prepared to handle it. When you tap into the guidelines of His Word, you are on the right path to understanding. We can be alerted to every scheme if we will listen to God's spirit within us. So, how do you know when you are under attack? Number one, when persons are under attack, they lose their spiritual hunger for God. How do you become spiritually hungry? How do you stay spiritually hungry? You have to learn how to talk to yourself and tell yourself how to think. That is how you take control of your mind and teach it how to flow with the Word of God. The second thing that happens to a person under attack is a loss of strength. The third way to recognize an attack is that you don't feel like yourself. How do you survive such attacks?

Weapon #1 Liardon quotes Ephesians 6: 13. *Put on the whole armor of God.*

Weapon #2 In Ephesians 5 Paul says ...*be filled with the Spirit by speaking to yourself in psalms and hymns and spiritual songs.* Most individuals for some reason are nurturing hurts and wounds. I also was that person. Remember, though, a nurtured memory under attack has lost confidence and trust in God. If we continue on this path for very long, we will lose the soundness of our minds. According to Liardon, mental wards are filled with hopeless victims, put there from nurtured hurts and wounds. In many, the sole source was a hurt left unresolved. Medication will not heal the hurt; it can only paralyze a memory. Liardon further reminds us of a key point in life. "Truth is the only antidote for deception." Always remember the words of St. Paul in Philippians 3: 13...*but this one thing I do, forgetting those things which are behind, and reaching forth unto those things which are before.*

1982 Rochelle & Chuckie
Play Music and Play Ball!

1983 Tommy Edwards
had its own baseball team

World Famous
photo taken by Tommy Edwards
of Elvis and Bill Haley in 1955

1978 Chuck on Drums

1991 Dion and Chuck

CHAPTER 9

TOMMY EDWARDS RECORDS: A CLEVELAND MUSIC TRADITION SINCE 1962

Consider the lilies of the field, how they grow, they toil not, neither do they spin. Matthew 6: 28.

Always give thanks for everything to our God and Father in the name of our Lord Jesus Christ. Ephesians 5: 20.

In addition to trying to re-boot my thought processes, I was still faced with the real question of how I was going to support my wife and children now. Remember, at this stage of our life, mine was the only income that was supporting our family. Michele was working at Tommy Edwards Records to help develop her financial skills from July of 1982 until around the fall of 1985. Because of the stress with our marriage situation, she chose to resign her position.

After leaving RB&W around Halloween of 1985, I knew I was in no physical or mental state to assume any type of career position. I was still angry about my plight. Work so hard at doing the right thing, and is this what you get in return? I met with a few attorneys about taking legal action against ADC. One suggested applying for Worker's Compensation since I was not able to perform the same work I excelled in for over a decade. Was I seeking justice or vengeance? Clearly, I filed a Worker's Compensation case to try to obtain some justice for what was done to me and to my family. To file such a claim I knew would not only be embarrassing but a long, hard fight. But I also knew that the situation in which I was placed in June of 1985 was unethical and morally wrong. And after I had tried to "pick myself up by my bootstraps" by resuming my career in a similar field with RB&W, I knew all that I had studied for, worked for and developed was finished. I would never work again in that field.

The fact of the matter remained, what now? Out of everything bad is supposed to come good. Well, Michele leaving the store was bad. But maybe it gave me somewhere to go until I was in a position to go somewhere better. So, that was good.

In March 1986, I started trying to "do something" to occupy my mind from the other calamities that were occurring. And that something was spending time at Tommy Edwards Records. I can still recall that I would spend less than an hour in the store before I would get either anxious or mad and have to leave. One of my first tasks was to assume some of Michele's old duties, paying the bills. It would take me forever simply to try to write out one check. That's how confused my state of mind was at the time. One thing I did not plan for was the backlash such a decision would bring me. Pat, my editor, talks about what she calls her "Balcony People." Those are the individuals who support you no matter what. They know you are trying your best, and they offer their positive support because they think you deserve it. They are of great value at times such as I was muddling through.

Now, please remember, to some in my inner circle I was a whiz kid. This is my ego speaking, but facts are facts: I had achieved all I had set out do. So, when you think those that know and love you will support you in your time of need; when you think that those who have watched you walk the walk will support you in your time of need; when you think that anyone in their right mind can decipher the pain and suffering you are going through, don't count on them! Count on Him!

As easy as that is to say, it still hurts to think that even your innermost circle of friends and family will judge you when you fall. People say things that hurt you, and for the most part, they may not mean to hurt you or realize that their words are harmful. But, at least with me, words linger and last.

I am the type of person who needs positive reinforcement as is the case with most individuals going through any form of depression or trying time. If you know persons traveling through deep waters, please put a guard at your mouth and think before you speak. Better yet, pray before you speak.

What does Scripture say about "the tongue"? *Death and life are in the power of the tongue and those who love it will eat its fruit.* Proverbs 1: 4.

A gentle answer turns away wrath, but a harsh word stirs up anger. Proverbs 15: 1.

A soothing tongue is a tree of life, but perverseness in it breaks the spirit. Proverbs 15: 4.

So, what's my point? Well, two of the remarks I heard when I was struggling just to move every day that still linger are "You're going to run a rinky-dink record store? You were a vice president." "It's bad enough you don't love your wife anymore. Now, you don't even want your children."

There also was a Christian preacher who made a very important statement: "If you find yourself around negative people, don't walk away from them. RUN!" Wise man! Wise man! As hard as it may seem, sometimes your loved ones are the first ones you have to run away from temporarily.

In addition to the spiritual side, I was lucky to possess an Italian side that was made of inner toughness. Did you ever see the great 1993 movie, *Bronx Tale*, starring Robert DeNiro? If not, rent or buy it. My favorite scene in it involves the father (DeNiro) trying to pull his son away from the negative influences of the neighborhood. The mob boss has taken a liking to the boy because he didn't rat him out. So, DeNiro goes in the bar and takes his son away from the environment he wishes him not to be around. As they are walking out, his son yells at him, "The working man's a sucker, Pop!" Pointing through the window at the guys in the bar, he defends how good those guys are, how tough those guys are!

"TOUGH," DeNiro shouts. "I'll tell you who the real tough guys are. The dads who get up each and every morning to go to work to support their families. That's the tough guys!"

That's something of the example I have to look back upon with my own father. He was raised in a similar neighborhood as in the movie. Most of his friends walked the tough guy walk, but he chose, even though divorced, to be the real tough guy and support his two children, both financially and emotionally. This may have been a link to my choosing to carry on in my times of deep waters. Life may have been unfair to me, yet his example was there to reflect upon. He made a choice. I am sure it was not an easy one. Now, I was faced with a similar one. Was I prepared to do the right thing?

I am fortunate enough to have been raised in neighborhoods at both ends of the spectrum. In one environment, I learned the wholesomeness of middle-class America and in the other that you had to be tough in thought and action to survive in this world. Little did I know that both would aid me in my journey through life.

Another saying is "You have to hit rock bottom before you can get better." In other words, the only way God gets some of our attention is when we are on our backs, looking up! I was at the point where I knew something was turning my life around, yet I lacked any spark. I was working my way back but was still fearful of every step!

Another turning point came when I wanted to take my kids to the park. Michele and I were still separated, and each of our families was trying to protect those they love.

When I called and asked, Michele refused to let me take our children to the park. So, I temporarily sank back to the couch for another trip into the past! Then, I got another idea. Ask Rochelle and Chuckie. Let them decide. I can still hear their little voices, shouting YES! As simple as that may seem, it was a monumental decision in my life. We went to the park and played baseball that day, a day I will never forget. My children gave me a spark that began urging me to trek on.

I can recall while attending St. Joseph's High School part of our required summer reading were two books, *Metamorphosis* and *Don Quixote.* The first had a very graphic photo on the front cover of a man whose head was that of an insect. Ever so slowly, he was evolving more and more into the insect. The second had a character on the cover of a tall, scraggly monk, who was a fighter for the right as he perceived it, even though he was misunderstood. Listen to the words of "The Impossible Dream" that describe the idealistic quest of Don Quixote in the musical *Man of LaMancha.*

During 1986, I felt a lot like the character in *Metamorphosis.* My body was way out of sync, and I was literally wrestling daily with good and evil. Each morning, as in *Metamorphosis,* I was scared to look into the mirror to see what creature I would be dealing with. Somehow I knew that not only my life wouldn't be the same, but I as a person would not be the same either. It was hard to face the facts.

Had I not devoted my life to studying, working and striving for "the best for my family"? Had I not devoted my energies to being the best person as I was trained and raised to be? The answer to both was an emphatic YES! Then why did my God allow this to happen to me? I was going through a metamorphosis of the Spirit! Come to think of it, I still am.

Once the smoke had cleared, I began putting what energy I had into running our record store, Tommy Edwards Records. The store was not doing as well as it had in the past. Sales were down nearly 50 percent in the past two years. So, like everything in my life then, I wanted out! I decided to sell the place.

Our dad had always taught us to save for a rainy day. In other words, no matter what you do, have at least six months of house payments in the bank. Like a good student, I did that. Just when I was beginning to sort out a "survival plan," the IRS decided that since our accountant did not check the box for a Sub-chapter S corporation, Rick and I both owed $10,000.00 for tax credits taken. The majority was for penalties and interest

Ricky was living in Rochester, New York, at the time. He simply went into his local office and explained the facts. They said it was common sense of the intent of our company, and no such taxes or penalties were due. Armed with his paperwork from the New York office, I marched into our local office. When I showed them Rick had been forgiven of any such obligation, the reply was "We don't care what they do in New York. This is Cleveland, and you owe the money." Before I could react, they attached our personal bank account and stole nearly $10,000.00. Our six-month nest egg for a rainy day was gone!

As a last-ditch effort, Michele called her cousin, George Slyman, my old boss at Accurate Die Casting, to inquire if he could help her and her family. Financially, we were dry. She told him that I had over $50,000 in Accurate Die Casting's salaried pension plan. Could Cousin George intervene and obtain such funds to keep our family going? His reply, "I'll pray for you, Cuz."

To add insult to injury, while shoveling snow, I had this loud bang in my left ear and blood was coming from it. I had a broken eardrum.

Even though 1986 was an awakening point in my life, it still was a daily battle. With all our funds gone, no prospect of a renewed salary of the recent past, I thought it best to re-group and start over. Michele and I had our differences, and there were lawyers for divorce proceedings. There were a few months that things got so bad I chose to leave the house for fear of the daily disagreements and no movement by either Michele or myself. I finally got enough strength to call a realtor and put our custom home on the market.

There were some positive efforts by our friends and prayer partners, the Wrobels, to try to get us back together. These will be described in Chapter 10. Jerry and Grace interceded with their own manner of marriage counseling. Mostly through their efforts, Michele and I stopped the war.

On another front, we had a buyer for Tommy Edwards Records, and we had a buyer for our home. Although it took awhile, through the aid of an attorney we beat the IRS. Sixty percent of our money was returned without any interest, penalties or legal fees.

Even though we had a qualified buyer for Tommy Edwards Records, I decided that I needed a place to go and "Tommy" was it. We did not sell. Besides, I seem to love any organization that has a rich and deep history. Tommy had that. Not only was Tommy Edwards a prominent figure in the radio field, he was the first to play, book, and photograph The King of Rock'n Roll in Cleveland, Elvis Presley. To learn of the store's rich history, you can visit www.tommyedwardsrecords.com.

In addition to spreading out into the entertainment field, Tommy Edwards Records started a softball team. Its real purpose came into play when I thought of holding fund-raising games starting with Jerry's Kids, Feed A Family, D.A.R.E., Make A Wish, and Cleveland's Rainbow Babies & Children's Hospital. Our team, Tommy Edwards Top Ten, won all ten tournaments from 1991 until 2000. We played the local radio and TV stations, even the Rock'n Roll Hall of Fame. We oldies even defeated my son's college buddies, real baseball jocks, in some very close games.

Over the years we have made friends with many local celebrity on-air personalities, Carl Reese, Bill Randle, Norm N. Nite, Chuck Collier, Carl Monday, Jeff Maynor, Big Chuck and Little John, and Barnaby. Carl Reese stands out as the real deal. He never came off as someone of importance although he has a legacy in the Cleveland radio and music market that is beyond compare.

In spite of the celebrities I met and the fund-raising for worthwhile causes, running a record store was a far cry from my previous position as vice president of a corporation.

Let me reiterate something I said earlier. I don't know why most of us expect the unexpected from our loved ones when we know that they have gone through a traumatic event in their lives. Like broken bones, they take time to mend. Broken hearts, broken minds and broken spirits require the same. But how do you expect outsiders to understand if only bodily injury is acceptable under the laws of Worker's Compensation. The first question my attorney for Worker's Compensation asked me was Did you receive any physical injury at the time of your claim? So, I started the long journey down the court system to see if we could find some form of financial restitution for our losses from Accurate.

In the interim, I had to make a real decision on What now? When it came to trying to go forward, I had to realize that, for now, my means of sanity and a way to make a living was the record store. It was very difficult for me to accept my newfound career. I struggled with what I felt was the unfairness of the situation.

I had worked very hard to climb the ladder of success But for this? Eventually, I was learning to guide my thoughts with Scripture. I tried to tell myself, "Do not be anxious. Your circumstances aren't your God!" Or in other words, *Be still and know that I am God.* Psalm 46: 10.

2000's Jerry Wrobel at the Sunday Prayer Meeting

2000's Grace Wrobel- Hands raised and all!

Patty Scraggs Hudec
1970'S PHOTO

Terry Drake

CHAPTER 10

*I GET BY WITH A LITTLE HELP FROM **HIS** FRIENDS*

Enter by the narrow gate; for wide is the gate and broad is the way that leads to destruction, and there are many who go in by it, Because narrow is the gate, and difficult is the way which leads to life, and there are few who find it. Matthew 7: 13-14.

When there is no vision, the people perish. Proverbs 29: 18.

When someone becomes a Christian, he becomes a brand new person inside. He is not the same anymore. A new life has begun! All things are from God who brought us back to himself through what Christ did. 2 Corinthians 5: 17.

They that wait upon the Lord shall renew their strength. They shall fly like eagles. Psalm 91.

During both 1985 and 1986, I got to a point, like Popeye, where it was "It's all I can stands. I can't stands no more." And like Curly from *The Three Stooges*, when he heard one word, Niagara Falls, he lost it, and Moe and Larry had to restrain him.

I had trigger points and trigger words. I needed help for my current state. We all have heard the term open-heart surgery; I went through open-mind surgery. It came in the form of three (the trinity) types of aid: The Twinsburg Prayer Group, Emotions Anonymous and Terry Drake.

The first was a group that I used to think of as poor souls with crutches, The Twinsburg Prayer Group. It was, and still is, led by Jerry and Grace Wrobel. Michele and I met them at St. Cosmos and Damien Catholic Church in Twinsburg, when all of our children were young. I had known of this prayer group for a number of years.

Since my promotion to vice-president in 1979, Michele had to assume much of the parenting at home. At that time, Rochelle was four and Chuckie was two. Weekends were great, and we spent the greater part of them doing things together. My fondest memories were Friday nights and Saturday mornings at Michele's father's restaurant, Dave's Place. It was less than a mile from our home, and it was in the center of downtown Twinsburg.

But Monday through Friday I was out of town, and Michele had a lot on her hands. Besides being a weekday single parent, she was working five to six days a week at Tommy Edwards Records as the bookkeeper. In 1981, some of the stresses of life began to engulf her. She was having anxiety attacks. Michele developed a form of agoraphobia, a fear of open or public spaces. So much so, that at one point, she was homebound. With the aid of a psychologist, she was working things out. The Wrobels offered spiritual assistance to her. Imagine how shocked I was to witness these so-called Catholics raising their hands in praise, speaking in tongues (that one freaked me out) and reading from their Bibles (imagine that!), and always quoting chapter and verse. Now, that was really foreign to me.

The first time I saw this was after a long, hard day at the office. I came home to no one. The note said, We're at the Wrobels. I drove to their house, about twenty houses down in the same development. When I pulled in their drive, there they were, praying over Michele with hands lifted. What the hell? I loved my wife dearly, but her state of mind was doing a number on mine, or so I thought. I somehow found a way to pull her out of there.

What was going on? Wasn't life stressful enough? Now my wife was looking for answers from "those born-agains!" They freaked me out. Don't get me wrong, I really enjoyed their company, as a family, but figured they must have had some real emotional issues to deal with. They were practicing Catholics, yet performed this weird form of worship. Now, they were using their voodoo methods on my family!

Who do you think I turned to when I was drowning in depression? My friend, Jerry Wrobel.

The Prayer Group

My name is Jerry, and my wife's name is Grace Wrobel. We both came from a traditional Catholic background. The prayer group began in our home in the early 1980s. Grace and I attended a retreat weekend and had a born-again experience. We encountered Jesus Christ and accepted him as our personal savior (John 3:3). It changed our lives dramatically. We started having Bible studies and eventually were introduced to the Charismatic Renewal that was engulfing the Catholic Church during the mid-1970s. It was the Pentecostal experience that emphasized the release of the Holy Spirit (Acts 2: 1-4). The Charismatic release stressed the importance of the gifts of the Holy Spirit. Healing was one of the gifts. We began praying for healing in our group and for a greater release of God's gifts. We believed that Charismatic prayer and the anointing of the HOLY SPIRIT could bring about healing and change in a person's life. We also believed that when Jesus came into a person's life, major changes took place and this happened only by the HOLY SPIRIT. It is by the HOLY SPIRIT that a person becomes born again. The regenerated man steps forward and the old man passes away. That is the man of sin. It is the beginning of a walk with Christ. Christian community was an important part of our life at that particular time and still is today.

It was about the same time that we met the Rambaldo family whose children attended St. Rita's Catholic School along with our children. It was the beginning of a close relationship between our families. Chuck and Michele and their children, Rochelle and Chuckie, lived on the same street. My son, David, and Chuckie were about the same age and became good friends. Michele would visit often, and soon Jesus became an important part of her life. When Chuck would come home from work, he would seem anxious and under a lot of stress. I would try to talk to him about how Jesus had changed my life, but he did not seem interested. As time went on, Chuck's situation grew worse. His job pressures resulted in Chuck becoming clinically depressed. I saw him become an angry person, and his depression impacted his family and put a terrific strain on their marriage.

During this time Chuck and Michele purchased a new home. The added financial pressure caused Chuck's situation to become worse. He moved to North Royalton to his new home but seemed even more unhappy. I would visit him and try to share Scripture with him and cheer him up. He would come to prayer meeting with Michele and was very desperate. In addition to his horrible job situation, Chuck and Michele's marriage was in trouble. In the prayer meetings, we would pray with Chuck and Michele, but their marriage seemed to be headed for divorce. I saw what seemed the power of God come upon an irreconcilable situation. Michele made a decision to try to save their marriage and drop the divorce proceedings. I knew it was the hand of God that intervened and saved what is today a beautiful family.

It was during this time that I witnessed Chuck become that NEW CREATION (2 Corinthians 5:17) that St. Paul talks about in Scripture. The Lord seemed to take Chuck to the bottom of the rung of the ladder so that He could build him up in His image and likeness. The corporate man became the man of Christ. What I saw in Chuck was no less than a miracle. And do not be conformed to this world but transformed by the renewing of your mind that you may prove what is good and acceptable and the perfect will of God. (Romans 12:2). Chuck today has the mind of Christ and exhibits the love of Christ. He truly is the work of the Holy Spirit. He is a family man, a good husband, and father. He has been healed and restored by God. Praise the Lord for He is faithful and good. Today Chuck is a powerful witness for the Lord Jesus Christ. He has come many times to our prayer meeting to share *his testimony with others. I can say I love Chuck as a brother. We are all brothers in Christ Jesus and, as Christians, share his resurrection.*

Another member of this prayer group, Marcia, was watching our family's plight all along. One day in 1986, Marcia called me and asked if I would meet her at a self-help meeting called EA. EA? What was that, I asked. I had tried so many different types of self-help and group meetings; I was getting a little tired of searching for another part of the puzzle.

My first meeting was April 30, 1986. For those of you who may not be aware of this fine organization, it was formed by a group of individuals who found a New Way of Life by working the Twelve Step Program of Alcoholics Anonymous, as adapted for people with emotional problems.

The Twelve Steps of EA;

1.) We admitted we were powerless over our emotions, that our lives had become unmanageable.
2.) Came to believe that a Power greater than ourselves could restore us to sanity.
3.) Made a decision to turn our will and our lives over to the care of God as we understand Him.
4.) Made a searching and fearless moral inventory of ourselves.
5.) Admitted to God, to ourselves, and to another human being the exact nature of our wrongs.
6.) Were entirely ready to have God remove all these defects of character.
7.) Humbly asked Him to remove our shortcomings.
8.) Made a list of all persons we had harmed, and became willing to make amends to them all.
9.) Made direct amends to such people, except when to do so would injure them or others.

10.) Continued to take personal inventory and when we were wrong, promptly admitted it.

11.) Sought through prayer and meditation to improve our conscious contact with God as we understood Him, praying only for knowledge of His will for us and the power to carry that out.

12.) Having had a spiritual awakening as the result of these steps, we tried to carry this message, and practice these principles in all our affairs.

Sitting in this arena of life was the best fit for my psyche at the time. As we introduced ourselves and members shared their individual emotional problems, I thought, Wow, these people are functioning in the real world, and they all have as serious, and in many cases, worse emotional problems than the Lord has allowed me to experience.

Hi, my name is_____, and I have an emotional problem. I'm a manic-depressive (bi-polar).

Hi, my name is_____, and I have an emotional problem. I am a schizophrenic.

Hi my name is_____, and I have an emotional problem. I have attempted suicide four times.

In the back of my EA book, I listed the names and phone numbers of 27 individuals with whom I sat around the table that evening. What I also recall that evening was the leader of the group, Loretta, who outlined what EA was all about. The fact that it believed and relied upon a Higher Power got my attention. The inside cover of the book explained Emotions Anonymous. As the paragraphs that followed explained, "You are invited to discover that EA fellowship of weekly meetings is warm and friendly"… and I still feel that warmth and friendliness as I type these words some two decades later.

What further struck me at the bottom of the page was The Serenity Prayer: God grant me the serenity to accept the things I cannot change, the courage to change the things I can, and the wisdom to know the difference.

Bingo!

At that first meeting I was also given an 8-page pamphlet. It detailed:

12 Helpful Concepts of the EA program

12 Just for today choices

Slogans we use

From Let go and let God to I have a Choice

The 12 Traditions of EA

And finally, the 12 Suggested Steps of Emotions Anonymous

Somehow, I knew at that first meeting, even before I said "Hello, my name is Chuck, and I have an emotional problem" that this was a place that would be a part of the puzzle that would help to get me back on track.

I looked forward to attending those Tuesday evening meetings. I felt that I was sharing and learning from the experts in our field. These souls did not have degrees hanging on the walls for all to see. Instead, they had their hearts on their sleeves and were holding them out to us.

As I write these words, my memory drifts back to those wonderful varied faces, those caring and sharing wonders. I pray that all who attend such meetings around the world receive the abundant return on their investment of time that I did.

If you wish to know more about this fine organization, call or write:

Emotions Anonymous
P.O. Box 4245
St. Paul, MN 55104-0245 U.S.A.

Phone (651) 647-1593
Fax (651) 647-1593
The website is emotionsanonymous.org

To find a meeting close to you, simply click on Meetings.

My tabulations of attended meetings show that I was faithful from April 30 through December 3, 1986. I returned in August 1989 for a few meetings, and I recall attending in 1992 with a group in Middleburg Heights at St. Paul's Church. I gave a short witness of my story that appeared in a book entitled *The Path to Serenity* (Minirth-Meier Clinic Series). (See Appendix.)

If you are ever in need of honest, open, sharing, caring, loving, warm, welcoming, God (Higher Power) believers, I don't care what state you're in, find an EA group. I can guarantee you that they will become a part of the puzzle that helps put you back together again.

It's been more than two decades since my interaction with EA, and I'm still learning that one of my weaknesses is to allow my emotions to surrender to what my gut feeling is telling me is not right. How come, you ask? I think it's a part of my "sins of the father" but in this case it's sins of my mother. There is no one else in my family who can love and be more understanding to all with whom she comes in contact. But with each strength, often there is a weakness. We are enablers. We are rescuers, especially where family is concerned. If someone is not making proper decisions or harming us, Mom always seems to find a reason or excuse for them. And unless I fight that emotional feel-sorry-for-them syndrome, I easily surrender to what my inner spirit tells me is wrong. Are you listening children, grandkids, and family? In analyzing some of my most successful worldly accomplishments, it is apparent that where I had to rely upon myself (and God), mission was accomplished. Where I allowed my emotions to overrule my mind, I either failed or worked through the situation, struggling with my emotions.

EA is a phenomenal organization that can help individuals like me. Break the habit. Break the family tradition! Visit an EA group near you.

Through Him we can have life and life more abundantly. John 10:10

The third part of my return to wellness involved Terry Drake. What an individual. For more than twenty years, Terry has always had an open-door policy for me and my family. God blessed me with an individual whom I could both relate to and learn from. Terry's recollections will give you an insight into our sessions.

Recollections of Chuck

Please be advised that this attempt at recalling events from years ago may be filled with a host of inaccuracies, particularly in regard to time frames and sequence of events. Also, in the years subsequent to Chuck's involvement with Southwest General Hospital I have become close to Chuck and his family. Therefore, there is a certain subjectivity inevitably coloring these recollections.

I do, however, have some clear memories of certain events from my initial involvement with Chuck. It is these that I will attempt to share here. I also think that with hindsight and getting to know Chuck over a long period of time, I have a better understanding of what was disabling him to such an extent back in 1985 and 1986.

At the time Chuck came to SWGH (Southwest General Hospital), I was working as a clinical social worker on our inpatient psychiatric unit. My job duties included providing a great deal of the family therapy done on the floor. I was also in charge of the "Partial Hospitalization Program", which was essentially an intensive day treatment program for patients who did not require inpatient treatment....but were ill enough that an hour a week with a therapist was just not enough.

Chuck was admitted to PHP by one of our better known physicians.

This particular doctor was somewhat renowned as a great diagnostician as well as a great pharmacologist. Bedside manner, however, was not his forte. One patient described him as having the warmth of Attila the Hun. For patients in need of talk therapy, he was not much assistance. He did, however, have the sound medical judgment to realize Chuck was in bad shape, and, as a result, he referred him to our program.

I also think the referral was made to us because Chuck did not want to come as an inpatient. His depression was such that he, no doubt, met the criteria for admission, but after an unpleasant ten days on St. Luke's inpatient unit, Chuck didn't want any part of it.

I first met Chuck in the morning "insight" group I would run for all the PHP patients. Usually, patients in PHP were fairly high-functioning people. Those who had been severely ill and doing better were placed in PHP as kind of an adjustment back to home and work. This wasn't the case with Chuck.

Chuck had not worked through any of his issues at St. Luke's. They were all still there, alive and painful. Chuck was somewhat unkempt, not by other patient standards, but by what I would later understand were Chuck's standards. His hair was not well combed. He needed a shave, and his clothes looked like he had been wearing them for more than a few days.

Chuck's facial expression was flat, showing little emotion, if any. He seemed removed, withdrawn, distracted….not fully connected to things around him. It was only when I sat down with him individually that he became more alive and then only after two or three days in the program.

When Chuck did start to talk, it seemed he was obsessed with recent events in his career. As I recall, Chuck was a wonder-boy on his job. He was a thirty-five-year-old vice president of labor relations for a good-sized Cleveland corporation. Chuck had been a success in everything that he ever had attempted—a pride to his parents, to his wife and children, to his community. He believed that where his world was concerned, everything could be conquered by hard work, a strong value system, and good intentions.

Chuck loved his job for the ten years he was at it. The early '80s were good economic times for Chuck's firm and for the employees that Chuck dealt with on a regular basis. His hard work benefited his career and it also benefited the people he worked hard to represent within the company. He acted in good faith and they gave him their trust and I would suspect their admiration as well.

But then times became more difficult for the company, and Chuck was asked to do things and provide information to the company employees that was untrue and that would ultimately work against them. He was caught. It was a moral dilemma with no "wins" in sight. Since it was his wife's cousin's company, it intensified the problem of divided loyalties among his extended family.

Chuck would go over and over and over the situation in his mind. He ended up quitting the company. He was unable to violate his ethics by lying to the employees, and he developed a smoldering resentment bordering on hatred for his wife's cousin whom he had considered family.

Chuck felt there was no direction he could take that was not a values violation. He could stay on the job, screw the employees and continue to stay in the graces of his extended family. In doing so, he could also continue to make the $100,000 income to which he and his immediate family had become accustomed. But he would not be able to live with himself.

The other option was to quit the job and risk not being able to support Michele and the two kids.

The lack of a viable alternative created a downward spiraling in Chuck's thoughts, emotions, and functioning. Added to this were intense financial pressures as well as family and marital problems.

With hindsight, I think part of what made Chuck's situation so intense was that he had never previously failed. Although he had seen a great deal of hardship, growing up in a tough section of town and in the military, Chuck had always stayed focused, stayed true to his values, worked hard and in that way he had succeeded.

He found the woman he loved at a young age, had two beautiful kids, a great career—and did it all by age thirty-five. Life was great, and he felt secure in his perception of the world. This was the first time he couldn't make something better—the first time he was asked to do something unscrupulous. The first time he didn't know what the hell to do.

I don't know how long Chuck and I met. Overall, I think it may have been two or three months. Chuck had gotten significantly better in about two or three weeks. He then went out and found another job almost identical to the one he had just left. It was his last attempt at trying to hang on to his career and to being all things to all people. He just couldn't do it. He quit after one or two days and was back with us for another month or two.

Part of the work I did with Chuck involved marital work as well as some work with the entire family. It was clear Chuck and Michele loved each other. That was never in doubt. However, they were angry and fearful in regards to what would happen to their lives. Meetings with them were loud and exasperating. There were disagreements about Chuck's decision to change careers, about where they would live and a whole slew of things.

I need to commend both Chuck and Michele that they were able to hang in there together despite the intensity of their disagreement, But they did. Ultimately, Chuck went into Tommy Edwards full time, and Michele, who had been a stay-at-home housewife, now had to seek employment. This was extremely hard for Michele to handle, but I think it became clear to her that Chuck just could not go back to the kind of work he was doing.

I believe that it was Michele's love and loyalty that eventually enabled

Chuck to recover. Their relationship eventually healed as decisions were made, but it was a long and loud process.

Chuck continued to visit me daily while in the program, and I was able to spend a great deal of time with him individually and in group meetings. As Chuck began to improve, there were signs of his real personality emerging. He became much more animated. His sadness now turned to occasional rage…whenever a certain cousin was mentioned. Most of all, I remember his humor. Chuck was always able to laugh at himself and his situation…once he got a sense of direction back in his life.

In the last month or so that I worked with Chuck, I could see his work ethic returning. The same energy he had used to be a success in business, he was now using to help himself get well. Chuck began attending EA (Emotions Anonymous) groups during the evening. These groups use a great deal of spirituality in their programs. I think this provided for Chuck the final piece for his recovery. It impressed upon him, more than I or the other therapists could, that we aren't in control of everything around us, that sometimes we can only do our best, and we need to work on accepting the outcomes…and making the most of them.

I could write much more regarding specific incidents or fragmented memories although I don't know how helpful that would be. Allow me to end with this, and if you have any questions, feel free to call me at any time.

Chuck doesn't know how to quit, and he isn't particularly great at compromise on issues that are important to him. He struggled with a major intensity to determine how he could stay healthy, stay true to his values, and yet support his young family. I noticed significant improvement in Chuck when he and Michele began to work through their differences. And there were differences!

As distraught and frustrated as both Michele and Chuck were, I never imagined either of them would ever quit. There was a lot of fighting, harsh words, (never abusive), high volume, tears and sadness, but there was always a strong connection as well. I know now that Chuck *did, indeed, have suicidal thoughts, but the point is, he never acted on them.*

I think Chuck and Michele both made a very brave decision to scuttle the life they had and risk it on a "rinky-dink" record store. God knows, it hasn't been easy, but they made it work. The kids are now great adults. Chuck and Michele have a strong and close relationship, and by very real standards, they've been quite successful.

I'm proud to know them both. In my line of work, it's not considered good form to blur the professional/personal boundary. This was one of the few instances in a twenty-five year career where I've done so, and this has occurred following Chuck's involvement at SWGH. I enjoy their company and have great respect for them as people.

It's people like the Rambaldos who make the work I do rewarding! If I can be of any further help, please call.

Terry Drake LISW

Strongsville Psychological Services
440.243.7780
Author's note: If you are ever in need of professional counseling, God will have blessed you if the individual He puts in your path is a counselor like Terry Drake.

1970's
Photo of Uncle Arnold and Cousin JoAnn (Paschull) Odell

CHAPTER 11

HOW GOOD IS GOOD ENOUGH? DUST YOUR FEET.

And whoever shall not receive you, nor hear your words, as you go out of that house or that city, shake the dust off of your feet.
Matthew 10: 14.

Don't imagine that I came to bring peace to the earth! No, rather a sword! I have come to set a man against his father, and a daughter against her mother—a man's worst enemies will be right in his own home. Matthew 10: 34-36.

For God did not give us a spirit of timidity, but a spirit of power, of love, and self discipline. 2 Timothy 1: 2.

If you are of the belief, or were taught to believe, that it is by our good works that we obtain eternal life, our eternal reward, how many good works are enough? In my quest to try to understand why He inspired me to share some things that at times are both very private and hard to put out for public display, a recurring theme in my mind is my deep love for those Christians known as Catholics.

For the past two decades I have experienced many doubting Thomases as I was, within my family and circle of friends. I have also learned in the writing of this book that the hardest person to bring to Christ is the good person. That's what I thought I had to be. Most of my family and friends have been raised that we get to heaven through our good works. Thus, they all strive to be good. I also have come to realize that as Christians we are all followers of Christ. It is my belief that there is no one true church. I don't believe in denominations.

Like my experience in the business world, I accepted differences of individuals regardless of their education or titles. I believe that all Christians have a need to vocalize their dependence on their Savior, the Lord Jesus Christ. I didn't believe, let alone know about, the vocalizing part until I did it. And worked!

In my reading, listening to cassettes and compact discs on the subject, one of the best I found is titled *Grace to You* by John MacArthur. He and his associates were trying to unify Christian believers. In their search they discovered that in his church they get five to ten Catholics weekly who are searching for an answer. When these Catholics give their testimony, they all say that the Catholic Church has all the authority. And as far as the forgiveness of sin, they never knew Christ. They never had the power of the Holy Spirit in their lives. MacArthur further states that he believes that the Catholic Church is the single most fertile ground for evangelism. These people know about Christ, know about the Bible, believe all that but do not know how to become Christian.

In John 17, Jesus prayed, *That they may all be one.* When John MacArthur asked ALL denominations the question, "Why should God admit you to heaven?" other denominations said, "Because Christ died for my sins"… "By the grace of God"…"Through faith in Christ alone"…"I trust in Christ as my savior." And when a Catholic woman was asked, she replied, "Because I'm good." Catholics are not instructed to reaffirm the gospel of Jesus or to affirm the person of Jesus Christ. But once you do that, He sends his Comforter, The Holy Spirit, who opens a new world to you.

Our pastor, Father Dale, of St. Anthony of Padua Church in Parma, Ohio, once gave a sermon that struck home with me. In addition, it planted a seed of hope that the Catholic Church has spiritual leaders that do send His messages in our day and age. He began his sermon with the question: What are we really looking for in life? He reviewed the gospel reading for that particular Sunday that centered around John the Baptist. John had spent his whole life looking for the meaning of life. He is the first among many in the gospels who will come to realize that the full meaning of life is found not just in the truth, but in Truth, Himself, Jesus Christ. How we were introduced to Jesus is uniquely our own story. For most of us, our coming to Christ has been a bit like awaking from sleep (possibly the term born again?). The point is that following Christ is a gradual process that will take, for most of us, the better part of our lives. So maybe the best advice that can be given is to be patient. I once heard someone say that faith rises slowly in the soul like home-baked bread. It reminds me that my relationship with Jesus will always take time.

Father Dale continued, "Yet the best news of the Gospel passage is that with having found Jesus, we often discover that it has been Jesus who has been seeking us all along." It is actually Jesus' penetrating question, 'What are you seeking?' that really stirred Jesus' followers' souls to life. Jesus basically asks the same question about seeking the deeper meaning behind the life of Nicodemus, The Pharisee, the Samaritan woman, the man born blind, the woman caught in adultery, the lame man at the pool, and the family of Lazarus. "If by chance you found the cure for cancer, would you keep it to yourself? I suspect you wouldn't. What if you were to find the very secret to a full and meaningful endless life? Wouldn't you want to share it with others? So if you have a deep and abiding relationship with Jesus, tell somebody. Share the good news. We are surrounded by others who are seeking the very same thing and, sadly, they more than likely may not even know where to begin to find the answer. Besides, seeing them finally 'get it' is the only joy greater than getting it yourself." Thank you, Father Dale!

The Beatles weren't my favorite English group. But, as I get older, I realize that those guys, John Lennon and Paul McCartney, were gifted writers. The title of one tune, "I'm Looking Through You," pretty much sums up what the Holy Spirit allows us to see. Jesus called The Holy Spirit by two names—Comforter and the Source of all Truth.

When The Beatles sang "I'm looking through you," they were talking about how they thought they knew someone and, in time, finally realized that what they thought they knew, they did not know. With wisdom, they were able to look through the person and see the true spirit that was within. That is exactly what I was missing and did not realize it by being only two-dimensional: Mind, Body, but no Spirit.

That is exactly what Jesus gives us when we accept Him as our Savior. I did not realize it while struggling through my "identity crisis," but going to hell really gets you to heaven. Once you are sent the Holy Spirit, there is a comfort, an inner peace, a contentment that makes the serenity prayer a reality. In addition, He provides you with a Spirit that deceivers don't get. He allows you to decipher the Truth. This helps make your family, personal and business relationships easier but at times a bit harder. I am not saying it makes your life a cakewalk. Hardly. But The Holy Spirit provides you with discernment that makes your choices more correct, more fulfilling for you, and lets you be more at peace with yourself. This is the gift that I pray I can share with my loved ones, my friends, anyone I come into contact with. We spend most of our lives trying to solve problems. He gives us The Comforter, who provides the key to solving them with astute wisdom, while allowing us to live at peace with those things we can and cannot solve! Bread sang a song, "I would give anything I own just to have you back again." When you receive the gift of the Holy Spirit, you develop relationships that make you at peace, even when the Lord calls your loved ones home.

Speaking of loved ones, I got myself into trouble by assuming we all believed the same things when it came to unconditional love, doing the right thing and being a Christian. Remember, most of us were trained that being good equals eternal reward. So, why would someone not follow suit when dealing with the closest people in the world, their family? What further complicates the matter is that when we marry, we accept and respect our spouse's family as ours. We were also trained to respect our elders. Now, you are hooked emotionally if you buy into all of the above. The problem occurs when we expect more of individuals in our outside world than our own family. And there's a fine line to cross, as most of us know, when we are dealing with our spouse's family.

Please re-read Matthew 10: 34-39. For the most part, persons in the family may become off limits. It may be OK for them to disrupt your household, or for them to say things that are offensive, mean or downright distorted. Yet, we as Christians are expected to turn the other cheek. Well, as life sometimes teaches us, eventually such a uniform belief can hurt you! Remember, many of us were raised to "be the bigger person." Well, I can tell you from experience that there is a fine line between being the good Christian and becoming a victim for life, specifically when it comes to family.

Agreeing with family, immediate or in-laws, on what we feel is right and on doing the right thing is one of the most difficult situations you may face. I don't think any of us willfully intends to harm our loved ones, physically or verbally, unless we are really sick and in need of professional help. But because of our involvement with family, it is natural to try to aid, offer advice or point out paths that may make their lives a bit easier. Believe me, I have tried and failed on many, many occasions.

But if your heart is truly in the right place (trying to understand and live what God wants for you and members of your family) you must try. You must try with unconditional love. You must offer His guidance through His Word, and when you have wronged someone, ask forgiveness. For me, it's all about repentance. But you must remember that ultimately it's not your choice! Matters of emotional ties may involve a mother or a father, son or daughter, a spiritual or business leader. When you are tested in these circumstances, instead of filling just a cavity, try doing some root canal work. When you turn your life over to Jesus Christ as your

Lord and Savior, you are a new creation in Christ. And that new creation begins to develop an urgency, a new spirit, which compels you to speak out "as bold as lions!"

Part of my personality was always trying to make things right, trying to see the good in everyone, trying not to be trying! My mother has this same quality. I may have developed some of my instincts by listening and watching her. She is an angel, but we are walking on the devil's earth. As I have tried to "walk the walk," I am also called to "talk the talk." When Jesus proclaimed, "Go and make disciples of all nations," that included family. We have all heard of or been accused of being one of those "born-agains," people who are too pushy, too judgmental, too open about sharing "the truth," too quick to meddle in others' personal affairs.

A while back there was a popular Christian saying that asked us, when faced with hard decisions, "What Would Jesus Do?" Do the things we are hearing, actions we are seeing, the talk we are listening to align to the Word of God? If not, we are called to be bold as lions (Proverbs 28: 1) and speak out. Speak the truth, His truth, not the world's truth but God's truth in love! Not because we want to be known for being wise, not because we want those around us to see how "right" we are, but because, as His servant, we are compelled to share The Word.

You know that when you allow yourself to become emotionally involved with others, it takes effort. Normally, it's an effort that few seek to pursue. It's an effort that could cost you a friendship, cost you the association of a family member or members, cost you financially, cost you many sleepless nights. But simply to wash your hands of a situation as Pilate did or to pretend that everything is beautiful is not what Jesus calls us to do. We are to witness for Him, even when it hurts us. Always remember His words, *Pick up thy cross and follow me daily.* Luke 9: 23.

I will tell you that inner voice, the Holy Spirit, will help you to decipher what is right. And sometimes it may be the hardest choice. It may be very hard for you to break those emotional ties, but focus your attention and strength on your real ties, your spiritual ties. It takes a lot of practice, but once you switch gears, He will allow you to see more clearly.

Joel Osteen, the popular TV preacher, said, "There is much grace for family members starting their walk with God." He pointed out that it was a bit easy for him. His grandfather and his father were both renowned preachers of the Word. He grew up in and with the Word. "But to those who choose to change the path of your family, His grace will be passed on for many generations of your family." This walk has been difficult for me. My search for His truth was like trying to find a needle in a haystack. I did not have someone planting those seeds of life until age thirty-five.

On numerous occasions, Michele and I have been accused of not being Christian. Or, "You born-agains are so judgmental". Or "You call yourselves Christians?" "You are supposed to forgive." What does God tell us? Judge not yet ye be judged. Turn the other cheek. As hard as it seems, don't allow people to make you buy into this emotional dependence trap. Remember, on Calvary, there were two other individuals condemned to death. The one turned to Jesus and asked forgiveness, and Jesus replied, *Today you will be with me in paradise.* Luke 23: 43. Look at the word: Today! He did not say after your stay in purgatory. Or after your loved ones pray you into heaven. He simply said, "Today."

The other sinner did not repent, nor did Jesus grant him forgiveness. He did not turn to him and ask him, "What say ye?" One made the choice. The other, simply by his silence, made his choice. Always quote Luke 17: 3-4 when faced with emotional ties: *Rebuke your brother if he sins, and forgive him if he is sorry. Even if he wrongs you seven times a day and each time turns again and asks forgiveness, forgive him.* These are Jesus' words on forgiveness.

Don't become a victim of family emotional ties, family-impaired judgments passed on from generation to generation, or any other emotional baggage that will eventually drag you down. Because I can tell you from experience, those same individuals whom you listened to won't be around to mend your wounds; they are too busy passing that crap on to another unsuspecting victim. And don't ever allow anyone to tear you down or work on making you feel inferior or try to destroy your self-esteem. We are not called to be doormats for our Christianity. Stand up for yourself, and He will stand by you. We have a cousin we went to school with, raised our kids with and with whom we shared our problems. The time came for that family to act as Christians with regards to their child who was getting married against their will. Because their offspring came to us for help and guidance, we went to the parents in love to share with them what we felt as parents and as Christians we were called to do. They chose otherwise. They also chose to ignore us at any family function we attended. At first, most of their family was shocked at their conduct. These "family members" chose to ignore and walk by anyone who supported their daughter's wedding. But I learned that was part of their family culture. They know what is right. They speak out to their loved ones. And when the choice is made, they take the heat for awhile. Then, because "it's family," they allow these non-repentant family members to slip back into the family's graces.

In the words of Rodney King, "Can't we all just get along?" So, our cousins chose to overlook or forget about the matter. We, on the other hand, knew that to have true healing, forgiveness must take place. They were offered a few opportunities to make things right, but they repeatedly chose not to do so. At first, members of our family began to criticize us for not forgiving them. When I addressed it at a family gathering, the other family members pounced on me for my behavior. I acknowledged it wasn't the proper time, but it was my time. I apologized and stated that asking forgiveness was what was lacking in the make-up of certain members of their family. By now, I ought to know, I have been in and around it for forty years.

Another family member, the one who wronged my family back in 1985, chose the same path. No repentance. None whatsoever. God called him in 2000. I tell you that in the same way, there will be more joy in heaven over one sinner who repents than over ninety-nine righteous persons who need no repentance. Luke 15: 7. Recently, God has challenged my own family (my mother and brother) to a similar test that I lived and witnessed with Michele's family back in 1985. Sad to say, our strength as a family has been weakened from what I consider a difference of priorities of life. The lesson I had to learn back in '85 was that my priorities were out of line. Now I know God is first, then, family, and then business! I pray that other members of my immediate family learn the same lesson I did. I can tell you from experience that when you are not of the same yolk, choices become very different and difficult for an extended period of time. I have had to pray for Divine intervention when it came to matters of the heart.

When I questioned my nephew, Richard, as to why he changed his emphatic belief against one of my kid's choices, he replied, "I spoke out of love. I stated my belief, my opinion, but when they made a choice. I supported the decision. They're family!" And with family, sometimes it becomes very hard to decipher the truth in certain situations. Not because we don't normally have that ability, but because there is that emotional attachment of family involved. I heard another great line in another movie. *The Da Vinci Code*. In her analysis of a family matter, the main female character simply put it, "We are who we protect! What we stand up for." Think about it. Recently one of my brothers-in-law, wanting the family to heal, asked his cousin if he would call us and simply say, "Let's forget the past and go forward." That form of apology (repentance) would have been accepted.

Yet, the reply was, "I don't think I can do that." And he did not. My brother-in-law's reaction was total disbelief. The feud continues but only on their side. We have asked the Lord to forgive them for us, ("Father, forgive them for they know not what they do.") and we have accepted the fact that they choose not to have us in their lives—all over a matter of pride. Yet, it has been more than eight years, and I do not foresee a healing. They might choose to ride this into Jesusville! Their first cousin did!

There is another saying, "Talk is cheap." I can recall all the "talk" I heard over the years about the importance of family. But these same family members have chosen to talk to my wife only twice in the past eight years—at her father's funeral and at our son-in-law Mat's funeral. I guess some families know how to love in death but not in life. Or are they just hypocrites? The definition of a hypocrite is a person who puts on a false appearance of virtue or religion. So, in analysis of the situation, their talk is cheap and by their actions, appears to fit the definition.

Philip Yancey, in his book *What's So Amazing About Grace?* states: "Like a spiritual defect encoded in the family DNA, ungrace gets passed on in an unbroken chain. Ungrace does work quietly and lethally, like a poisonous undetectable gas. The toxin steals on, from generation to generation."

In my family, I have had to experience the hard way that we do not all see things eye to eye. I realize that some of their priorities in life, like mine used to be, are upside down. But, just as I thought The Twinsburg Prayer Group had emotional problems, I believe some of my family members view my thought processes as such. When people are blind to God's truths, it's truly hard to deal with the fact that they often just don't "get it." Sometimes it's a cultural thing, sometimes it's a certain mental disorder a family member may have and sometimes it's just plain pride. Whatever it is or whoever it is, no one is exempt from God's laws. If you follow Scripture and there is no healing, you have done your best. You are not to overlook real evil that exists just because it's family. It may be a hard battle. You most likely will be singled out as the problem. But in the long run you may be breaking a family tradition that God wants broken. *My grace is sufficient for thee. For my strength is made perfect in weakness. Most gladly therefore will I rather glory in my infirmities that the power of Christ may rest upon me. Therefore, I take pleasures in infirmities, in reproaches, in necessities, persecutions, in distresses for Christ's sake. For when I am weak then I am strong. 2 Corinthians 12: 9-10.*

There is another scripture I have grown fond of over the years while I wrestled with trying to break my habit of going to the extreme, striving to be a good person and a good Christian. That's *Shake the dust off your feet.* Matthew 10: 14. If you go to someone out of love or if someone offends you and you try to reconcile with them and they rebuke you or ignore you or choose to go against God's word, simply dust your feet. Walk on, knowing that it is for your betterment that you are not around such individuals. Remember how our Savior ended up on this earth? He was not loved by all. Surely, many chose to ignore him. Surely, his own people crucified Him! Your job is to simply be a seed planter. It's others' choice. He also teaches us in Scripture, *If any man will come after me, let him deny himself, and take up his cross daily, and follow me.* Luke 9: 23.

Please read the part often where He says, Take up His cross daily. We are called to plant the seeds but not to make sure that everyone in our life's path gets His message. With my life, it was a choice—a choice I ran from, a choice I chose to ignore—but a choice I finally made. Many seed-planters were sent by God to me. In time, I got the message. And that will most likely be your calling for many, many individuals whom you love. Plant the seed. It's up to each individual if it takes root. As much as I have many loved ones I pray for or for whom I drop simple seeds of faith, I do not see too many taking root. Yet, it is in His time not ours. Who knows? I may be with the Lord when some of the seeds from this book take root. Our job is to continue to spread His word and pray that it makes someone's life a bit easier, happier, more fulfilling while wanting to begin planting seeds of their own.

1992
The Crash

CHAPTER 12

THE PATH TO SERENITY: 1992

The righteous cry out, and the LORD hears, and delivers them out of all their troubles. Psalms 34: 17

Don't copy the behavior and customs of this world, but be a new and different person with a fresh newness with all you do and think. Then you will learn from your own experience how His ways will really satisfy you. Romans 12: 2.

Back to our world and our family life. Rochelle and Chuckie excelled in school. After attending St. Rita's Elementary School in Solon, they both attended Notre Dame Cathedral Latin High School in Chardon.

After the destruction of 1985 and 1986, Michele and I had to rent a family member's house in Solon from 1986 until 1989. By then we were in a better financial situation to apply for a home loan.

By 1987, the neighborhood where Tommy Edwards Records had been for twenty-plus years was aging and going downhill. So, we studied the market, and there was a new huge strip mall going up a few miles away, right off the freeway. As we all know, in business it's all about location, location, location. When we crunched the numbers, we would have to double our monthly sales just to break even. We chose to take the gamble and move the store. We had paid off the first bank note that had an interest rate of 22½ percent. It's amazing the courage that youth gives us.

It took over three months just to move all the records out (45s and albums). In addition, the market was changing and compact discs, which first came out in 1982, were becoming affordable.

We had to invest additional capital into the new trends in music, compact discs, cassettes, cassette singles, soundtracks. We were fortunate enough to be located right next door to an eight-complex cinema. The only problem was the owners did not build the theaters until one year after we opened. Once again we had to get creative, advertise more on radio, and do in-store events with local performers or oldies acts; the performers either signed their new compact discs or performed live. We even built a stage in the store. It paid off. Sales more than doubled.

Tommy Edwards and the Rambaldo family have always supported local talent. The relationship has been beneficial to all concerned. To date, we have produced more than ten Cleveland Local Legends compact discs with the expert aid of Mike and Gina Criscione.

Even though my business world was starting to regain some normalcy, I still was tuned into being fed His word. One day while I was driving to work, I was listening to Minirth-Meir, a ministry that did a daily show dealing with depression and anti-depressants. They mentioned that they were putting a new book together, *The Path to Serenity*, and they were seeking real stories from their listeners all over the country on how The Twelve-Step Recovery program changed their lives.

WOW! The lights went off in my head. I visualized mine being one of the stories they would select. I went to work that day and wrote a part of my story and sent it off.

In September 1991, I got a letter from Richard Fowler, Director of Minirth-Meir Clinic Services, stating, "Of all the hundreds of stories submitted for the book, yours was chosen to be used. (We only had room for seventeen stories). Thank you for sharing with us and the world what God has done in your life." After the words sank in, I was elated. I know the thought of writing this book took hold that very day.

When the book came out, on my birthday, February 12, 1992, I bought copies for all of my family, and second, I made a point to go back to an EA meeting and share.

The third thing that happened that showed me how fragile life can be was on February 13, the very next day. I was driving to work after a meeting in Twinsburg. It was around 10:00 a.m. and there was a slight freezing rain as I left McDonald's to turn onto the entrance ramp to the freeway.

Within a matter of minutes, I was facing death. We've all heard how some people's lives have changed in a blink of an eye. Well, mine sure did that day. While I was doing around 55 to 65 mph, I noticed a pick-up truck pass me in the fast lane and sort of do a fishtail. My first thought was What a nut, playing around in the morning on a freeway. Maybe he had been drinking was my only rational thought. Best to keep away. Immediately after that, I realized what his problem was, and I had the same problem. We were driving on black ice! The black Chevy Blazer that I was driving began to do the same dance as the other guy's truck. Being an ex-military man, I quickly remembered, don't panic. Turn into the direction of the slide. I did that. Something was wrong with the picture I was witnessing. Instead of slowly coming out of the slide, I was barreling towards a 5-foot snowy embankment that divided both sides of the freeway.

And it's true, everything seemed to be in slow motion! I remember thinking, my God, this could be it! What about Michele, Rochelle and Chuckie? I will never get a chance to say goodbye and tell them how much I love them and how much they have meant to me. Then another instantaneous thought occurred…What if I survived but was paralyzed? I am almost sure I did not have my seatbelt on. I wished I had taken the time to buckle up. Too late now. I can still visualize myself, holding tightly onto the steering wheel and heading directly into the snow-covered knoll.

Then CRASH! BOOM! BANG!!!

The next thing I knew I was standing outside of my beat-up SUV. The top of the vehicle was smashed down. The rear window had blown out, and the front windshield was smashed. There I stood, viewing the scene, almost as a spectator. I do not ever recall opening the door to get out of the truck. I knew it flipped over and over at least two times, possibly three.

When the police arrived, the officer looked at my wrecked vehicle and said, "You aren't the driver, are you?"

"Yeah." I replied warily as the combination of rain and ice fell on our heads.

"You're a lucky guy. I would say in 85 to 90 percent of these kinds of accidents, we put the driver in a body bag."

Those words shook me even more. God had his hand on me that morning. They say when it's your time, it's your time. That rainy-icy, dreary day was not to be the last one for me. Thank God!

August 23, 1992, was a day I shall not soon forget. It was a nice sunny morning. When I arrived at Tommy Edwards, Pat, a long time employee, had already opened up and was taking inventory. I was in the back office, ordering from one of our suppliers, when Pat came to inform me that there were two men out front who said that they were from The State of Ohio. That alone sent shivers down my body.

I gained my composure and went out to greet them. The one informed me that we were behind in our sales taxes and that they were there to shut our operations DOWN! Somehow, you just hear the words, and then disbelief sets in. I thought, No one called me. So I blurted that out. And they said that we had received numerous amounts of paperwork.

I replied, "Yeah, I know, and I have met with the local office on these issues."

"That's not our problem," was their reply.

Just then, our accountant walked in, saw what was going on, and walked out. He left us out to dry. I kept thinking, Dear God, who can I call? The one guy started putting yellow tags on the bins: Property of the State of Ohio. I called my brother and asked him what we should do.

"How much do they say we owe?" he asked.

"How much do they say?" he asked again

"$25,000.00 in taxes, penalties and interest."

Dead silence. Then, he simply said, "You're done!"

Strike Two, I thought.

My last hope was Ernie, the attorney. I phoned, and he answered, thank God!

I begged the boys to go get some coffee. They did.

Just then my father-in-law walked in and asked what was going on.

I simply said, "A misunderstanding." I am sure he heard that before, having operated his own restaurant, Dave's Place, for more than forty years.

Then who walks in? Ernie, the attorney.

He talks with the men from the state.

The one was adamant that we were out of business and that we should lock the doors and give them all the cash in the register. Thank God, the second one, who seemed to be in charge, had an open mind. I showed them the paperwork that I had sent and informed them that I had met with representatives from The State of Ohio. I explained the problem was simply that we had moved, and we did not know that we had to have a new tax ID number.

The tax returns that we were sending to Columbus were being credited to our old location.

A small technicality that almost put us out of business. Ernie called the lady who sent Stan and Bubba, the guys to do the dirty work. Ernie performed a miracle. She asked to talk to the two men.

They left with the stipulation that Ernie and I would meet with her the next day. I can still remember me driving us downtown and ranting and raving about the "injustice" of the entire situation. Matter of fact, as I relived the horror of the day, I got madder and madder and began to swear profusely.

Ernie looked at me and said, "Chuck, do you realize you are out of business? And if you continue with that profanity, how will you be able to conduct yourself as a professional with this lady?"

Well, when I have to be professional, I am professional. When I have to fight for my life, I am a prizefighter. I have been knocked down and gotten up so many times in the past twenty years, my back has a tattooed word on it: EVERLAST!

As I get older, I realize that life is like a boxing match. Sometimes you're in shape for the fight ahead. Sometimes you face an older opponent, sometimes a younger one. Sometimes your trainer or manager does you in. And sometimes you lose when you should have won. And many times you win when you should have lost. Those times of winning can be attributed to The Holy Spirit's divine intervention!

If you ever get involved with any form of government office or bureaucracy, you may win but you pay a price. The agreement was that the state would continue to investigate the matter. But in the interim, Tommy Edwards Records that had been paying sales tax for twenty years would have to bring in certified funds to the downtown office on the 23rd of each month. I DID THAT FOR TEN YEARS!

Just imagine building up enough cash to get certified funds and running downtown every 23rd of the month for a decade. No fun. And at times, very humiliating.

By 1996, this matter was still not settled, and I kept getting threatening letters from The State of Ohio. So, I went to Columbus and represented Tommy Edwards Records without legal counsel. The hearing took a few hours, and I could not get the lawyer who represented the State to sign an agreement on any figure. He agreed that Tommy Edwards did not owe the amount that the letters were stating, and that payments were credited to the wrong address. But to agree on a figure and resolve this issue was beyond his scope of authority. I kept asking In whose authority was it? As another Beatles' tune tells us, "No Reply". Frustrating, very frustrating. And I had taken time away from my business to drive down to the state capital.

In 1992, Tommy Edwards Records was celebrating its Thirtieth Anniversary. We worked with the local oldies' station, WMJI radio, and did many, many in-store events with national oldies acts including The Diamonds ("Little Darlin'"), The Spaniels ("Goodnight Sweetheart"), Frogman Henry ("Ain't Got No Home"), Lou Christie ("Lightnin') Strikes"), Len Barry ("The Bristol Stomp"), Joey Dee ("The Peppermint Twist"), Tommy James ("The Hanky Panky"), The Capris ("There's A Moon Out Tonight"), to name a few. The response was both profitable and phenomenal. We even produced a history of Tommy Edwards Records, "Legends in Our Time." It was the number one seller in our store.

Because of the radio and television coverage we received, we were invited to open a second location in downtown Cleveland. It was at this time that the Rock 'n Roll Hall of Fame was being built. We felt that it was not only an honor to be asked but an opportunity we couldn't pass up. So, I spent a lot of my time negotiating and then building our second location in one of Cleveland's oldest and most historic buildings, The Arcade. What a beautiful building. The owner of the building offered us a 90-day lease, to see if it would be worth our while to stay. He would pay the cost of the unit improvements, and we would simply pay rent. Such a deal.

We ran two locations during the holiday season of 1994, and business was good. Although it was extremely difficult to schedule employees, order stock, co-ordinate in-store appearances, and pay bills, it was worth it. When the end of 1994 came around, the Arcade's owner asked us to stay. He would offer us a one-year lease and once again would build our unit right off the main entrance on Euclid Avenue. With the Ridge Park Square location experiencing a decrease in annual sales, I felt that it was worth the effort, for downtown may have to become Tommy Edwards' new home.

Well, things went from bad to worse. The big box stores (Best Buy and Circuit City) opened in the spring of '95. We struggled to carry both businesses throughout the year. When the fall of '95 approached, I knew we had to close not only one location but BOTH! In addition, I had to negotiate a new lease in another city, Parma, with thoughts and aspirations that business would improve.

It's a good thing God gave us a lot of friends and family to help with the work. It was a costly ordeal. And as usual, brother Rick was there, along with Mom, Michele, Rochelle, and Chuckie, And also Cousin Joe, Big and Little Jim, Bill Ritz, Bob, VP of Moving, Slaby!

At forty-five years of age I was beginning to feel like a 45 rpm record, spinning round and round! I was honest with myself and said that maybe the best thing was to try to get Tommy going in the new location while seeking employment. I visited with a professional agency during Christmas of 1994. We put a resume together, and the first organization I sent it to was the one that seemed logical at the time, The Rock 'n Roll Hall of Fame. And to repeat the words of the Beatles, there was "No Reply".

I looked in the yellow pages for professional employment agencies. The one I visited with seemed good until we got to their fee— $2,800. NEXT!

Dennis Susnik, our accountant at the time and a fellow JCU grad, suggested a firm that helps clients not only develop a professional resume but also aids them in obtaining gainful employment. I knew he meant business when he wrote out a check to pay for the service. Wow!

Well, I was a bit nervous when I walked through the doors of that firm. The people seemed friendly enough. Together we produced a resume that "for sure" would put me back on top. Oh, by the way, did I inform you that they gave me a computer printout of possible leads? That's right. It was up to me to hunt down a firm that might be interested in my services. Then I would review my job search with them every so often. Boy, was I duped, along with probably thousands like me.

Being a creative person and with no responses from these so-called prospective firms, I began to check the Sunday *Plain Dealer* want ads. Another business associate referred me to another high-powered organization, "the best" in Cleveland. It turned out not only would they teach me to "RE-THINK" who I was, they would also spend a few weeks tearing me down to build me back up so that I would possess that confidence to "get the ultimate position." All for the low, low price of $8,000.00. Needless to say I made the decision not to accept their offer.

Back to the Sunday ads. Well, right there before my eyes, and I couldn't believe it, was the perfect position at the perfect place: Human Resource Director at John Carroll University. This truly was an act of God!

I could not wait until Monday morning to call. I won't bore you with the details, but I not only got a few interviews, I was also "the choice" of the individual I would be replacing. He was retiring, and thought that I was "the man for the job".

It turned out, however, that his supervisor did not share the same opinion. Well, live and learn. I was actively pursuing other avenues. In fact, I applied to sixty-three different places from December 1994 through January 2000.

Round Two. One of the last disappointing experiences once again occurred at my favorite institution, JCU. Securing a position there would mean a regular salary and also free tuition for both of our children. It was November of 1996. This time I saw the ad, once again, in the Sunday paper. It was for Alumni Director at John Carroll University. After meeting with and reviewing my qualifications with the individual I would be replacing, I was her choice. There came a day, after weeks of interviews, waiting and praying and hoping, the board was to make a decision. "Be assured," the outgoing director reminded me, "you are the choice, almost the sure bet."

When I phoned JCU's Alumni office, she informed me things did not go as planned. The board was not going to offer anyone the position. They were going to start the search all over again.

I pressed her as to what happened. "You said I was the sure bet."

She replied, "Are you ready for this?"

I certainly wasn't.

"Because you are a bit too old. They are looking for someone between thirty and thirty-five years old."

With disbelief, I informed her that if it wasn't for the fact of my love and fondness for JCU, an age discrimination suit was in order. As I type these sentences many years later, I am still in disbelief!

1994 Chuck and Chuckie,
from one of our last Turkey Bowl games

1995
Rochelle and Chuck played with their church's softball team

CHAPTER 13

JUSTICE: MAN'S OR GOD'S?

Trust in the Lord with all of your heart. Lean not upon your own understanding. Proverbs 3: 5.

A gentle answer turns away wrath, but a harsh word stirs up anger. Proverbs 15: 1.

By now, do you get the idea that I like movies? There is a movie starring Al Pacino that I am fond of, *Justice for All*. It depicts the corruption of our court systems. In the end, Pacino, the lawyer defending his rich, untouchable client, learns that he is guilty. His years of defending "the devil" finally got to him. In the summation, Pacino lets everyone know that there is no evidence to convict his client, but he has knowledge that he is guilty. After informing the court with proof of his client's guilt, who do you think the police carried out of court? That's right. Pacino.

Ernie Sobieski also reminds me how, when we were young, we looked for justice. We got excited when we thought that we had walked through the storm and finally found JUSTICE! But you have to learn that on this earth, we all have to deal with man's justice, not God's. Sometimes you win when you should have lost, and sometimes you lose when you should have won. But with God all things are possible. And it's in His time that we learn to surrender. It's hard as hell at times. The hits they just keep on coming!

In 1996, we were once again taking hits from this world that just kept on coming. If you ask Michele, she might depict it as "the year of the blizzard." Just when you lifted your head to see if that relentless cold was passing—BOOM! We got hit in the kisser again!

It all began at the end of 1995. The management group in the Parmatown Mall decided that "we didn't fit" even though we had a five-year lease. For more than two decades, Tommy Edwards had successfully found a way to pay its rent every month. The truth was that a major cell phone company was seeking retail space in their strip mall. There were no units vacant at the time. So, the powers that be decided to find a tenant that appears unable to make it or find grounds for eviction of one of the smaller tenants. They found us.

It was three days after Christmas that the mall's corporate lawyers had us in court. They were trying to invoke a clause of the more than 100-page lease that had to do with signage. When the judge called our name, he paused. "Tommy Edwards Records. Is that the record store that has been around forever?"

"Yes," we replied.

"Well, how much do you owe these people in back rent?" the judge questioned.

"Nothing," I replied.

"Let me remind you that you are in a court of law," the judge said sternly. He asked me the second time, "How much are you behind in rent?"

"Nothing," I replied again.

He lowered his glasses and asked their team of lawyers, "How much is Tommy Edwards Records behind in rent to you?"

"He is correct, your Honor. They are current at this time."

"Then why are we here?"

"We would like to invoke Section.... gobbledegook..."

The judge turned to the section and read it. "Are you sure that you want to evict these people on this clause?"

"Yes, your Honor," was their attorney's response. "The signage allows for 18 inches. They are two inches over the height limit!"

"Two inches?" He lowered his glasses once more and peered at the team of legal beagles. "Never in my twenty-five-plus years on the bench have I seen someone try to use such a technicality to evict a tenant."

There is a God, I thought!

He asked them once again, "Are you sure you want to invoke this?"

"Yes," was the reply. The judge swung his head around to us and said, "When can you get out?"

I only heard the word OUT!

"Out?" I said. "We have only been in for ten months! We have a 60-month lease."

He replied, "I don't care. The law is the law. You'll be out in 14 days."

 Some Christmas present!

Of course, we appealed. A lot of good that did us. The same judge was assigned the case. Case closed! And justice for all!

Well, when they say things seem to go from bad to worse, in 1996 that was the case. Since we had invested bucks into building our unit and had to tear it down in less than one year, do you think we recouped our investment that year? Now, we were like the song Frogman Henry sings, "Ain't Got No Home."

I was faced with having no home for Tommy, and Michele and I had two children attending our alma mater, John Carroll University. No retail facility meant there was no income, no job, and no near-prospects of finding Tommy another home!

Waking up on the morning of March 1, 1996, after storing all of

Tommy's inventory and store fixtures by 2:00 a.m., I realized that in a little over a year, we had torn down two 'Tommy Edwards' facilities, built a new one, and then torn that one down, too. What was the outlook?

Our son, Chuck, made the varsity baseball team at JCU in his freshman year, and was in Florida during March, 1996. We got a call from first him and then his coach that Chuck was starting to get sick. They did not know what it was but that he was seeing a doctor, and we should know soon. And we did. It was mono, and his coach was putting him on a plane for home. When I picked him up, I was shocked to see how sick he really was. Michele and I took him weekly to the Cleveland Clinic for intravenous injections. He was so weak and so down.

While we were tending to our one child, our other, Rochelle, even though she was excelling at JCU in her third year, thought that she could make more money as a waitress. She was working part-time and gobbling up the dough, or so she thought. She informed us, "I need a little time off. I am just going to drop out for a semester. I promise I'll go back next fall."

Well, after many family discussions, our strong-willed child chose to wait tables. She found a boyfriend, a cook at the place where she worked. Not exactly what Mom and Dad prayed for.

During 1996, the problems we were faced with started to look all too familiar. But this time, I was not fearful. This time I did not wake up every night worrying about my problems. This time I did not have to seek professional help. This time God showed me that it works. If you truly believe, truly trust, truly have turned your life over to Him—sweet surrender is just that.

If you do this, you are able to walk without falling. You are able to live the Serenity Prayer. You are at peace, yet you know that in past similar circumstances, you weren't. He prepared me for this storm during the past decade. I had studied His Word and given my life to Jesus Christ. Remember, *You can do all things through Jesus Christ who strengthens you.* Philippians 4:13

When the storms of life hit our family again, we were prepared to execute that which He had taught us. Instead of allowing my emotions to overtake me, I now know to rely on Him. I did not know how we would resolve the rough roads ahead, but I did know that I did not have to try and figure it out. Let go and let God. He always keeps His promises, and He never fails you!

I have to admit I was somewhat surprised at the way my inner man, the third dimension The Holy Spirit had given me, was operating. Instead of curling up on the couch, I was taking one day at a time. Please understand that these were not easy days. There were obstacles being thrown at us that we had no idea how to solve. Yet, I continued to have that inner peace, that deep knowledge that everything would be all right.

Next, the bank came a-calling. I had always assumed the role of financial head of the house. I made the house payments, kids' school payments, car payments, and insurance and health payments and so on. The same rang true for Tommy Edwards' monthly bills.

All of Tommy Edwards Records was in storage, in hopes of finding a new location. A new location? Most everyone advised me to take the kids out of that costly college and forget about ever going back into retail. It's over.

Well, it's not over until God says it is. And He was telling me something different. And in the words of one of our friends, Bill Ritz, "Is the cow still giving milk? If so, why kill the cow?" The bank started sending us notices that our house payment was past due. If we did not catch up, proceedings to foreclose would begin. Not only were our circumstances changing, but also the retail music industry was changing dramatically. The big box stores had moved into our area, Best Buy and Circuit City. They chose to have as their "loss leaders," items that would entice you to visit their location, compact discs. They sold them at wholesale prices. Forty percent of our business was gone the day they opened.

Well, what do you think happens when you are forced to close your business that is the main supplier of the family's income? Your lifeline for paying bills begins to dry up. Tommy Edwards Records was out of business from February 29, 1996, until November of that year.

Our small crew of Tommy Movers was tearing down the store we just built and putting all of our inventory and fixtures in storage. I pulled into our home driveway with a U-Haul around two o'clock that winter morning.

When I realized what dire straits my family was in, did I choose to go back to the couch? Did I choose to get depressed again? Did I think that I could get us out of this unplanned mess? No, I relied upon my experience gained through the prayer group, EA, and Bible study. Don't get me wrong. There were many anxious moments, many moments of anger, many moments of feeling how unjust this all was, and there were moments of self-pity. Please notice the word I chose: moments. When I felt myself going down that path I was headed back in 1985, now I was better prepared to fight those thoughts, better prepared to know what to do and that was to stay in His Word. I did not feel like reading Scripture, but I made myself read Scripture. It brought me that inner peace of which many speak when in turmoil.

Back to the real world. Tuition had to be paid. I thought of my talk with my dad about my wish to attend JCU. If he could find a way to get me into the university, surely I could pay for my children to go there.

Well, sitting out in the garage was our black beauty, a mint 1975 Corvette Stingray. I can't tell you how long I deliberated on the idea of selling it to pay the kids' tuition. One of my brothers-in-law, David, had asked what we were going to do. Michele and I asked him if he would lend us $10,000 and hold the title to the 'Vette as collateral. He told us he had to think it over. Think it over? Well, to his credit, he did lend us the money. Sometimes you have to think the unthinkable.

By February 29, Tommy Edwards Records was not only temporarily out of business but it also had no home and no prospective site. During the month of March, I was frantically negotiating for a new location. It was hard to answer questions like Where's your current location? You were in Parmatown, but that was for a year. Didn't you have a five-year lease? If you're not in operation, where are all the store's fixtures and inventory?

With some divine intervention and the aid of brother Rick, we were able to negotiate a new lease with DrugMart in Parma Heights. The old tenant had just been evicted, and it was up to me to tear down his four offices and to build another unit. With no capital or bank loans forthcoming, we were going to need another miracle. And such a miracle was in the works.

As for the bank note on our home, it took some real negotiating and trips to the corporate offices to work out an agreeable arrangement. Michele's other brother, Rick, was a real aid here. We had to put the house on the market at once and were praying it sold quickly. Once again, God heard our prayers. This may sound unreal, but when we called the local realtor, he said we would have to invest at least $5,000.00 in home repairs before he would even consider listing it. Being an individual of strong convictions, did I take his word as gospel? Hell, no! There was a new kid on the block—$2,000 Realty. Like Earl Scrib, who used to paint any car any color for $29.95, this company would sell any house any size, any color for just $2,000. Our good cousin, Joannie Fadel, who also was in real estate, said they wouldn't last a year, but guess who owns a $2,000 office today. Joannie has had more than her share of adversity in her life and handled it admirably. It's gratifying to see her successful in business.

Once again God heard our prayers. The representative for this realty company told us that she thought she had a buyer for our home. It was true. By the grace of God, someone had placed a bid that was too low on a home on the next block. The prospective buyer was eager to buy in our neighborhood. He gave us another miracle: That individual bought our home without a For Sale sign ever going up.

As for spiritual support from our church, a lot was left to be desired. When our pastor got wind of the financial difficulties we were facing, do you think he was the first to show up on our doorstep with support and words of encouragement? No way. Michele had been the bookkeeper for the church for more than three years. She had invited the pastor to our house on many occasions to enjoy her fine meals. His silence on emotional and spiritual support was replaced with a degree of human sinfulness. He began to make Michele's work life miserable. He thought it best she not handle large amounts of money due to the temptation it might bring. Talk about defamation of character.

Well, actions speak louder than words. Our spiritual leader was lacking in volumes. It wasn't bad enough that we were facing many battles, but the one individual from whom we might expect some understanding and divine wisdom displayed none. Worse yet, he demonstrated what we were experiencing from those OF the world. The only thing I can say is how disappointing it was for someone who professes to be a man of the cloth, a man of His word, not only to fail us but also the God he was supposed to be representing.

My mom's mother, Grandma Lucy—you'll recall she's the one who used to wash Rick's and my faces with Fels-Naptha soap—used to tell my mother that the priest was representing God when he was on the altar. The rest of the time he was just like us, a mere man. Grandma Lucy's wisdom.

Yet, through disappointment after disappointment, God kept reminding me that "it works"—surrendering your life to Him and persisting in stepping out in faith. He does give you the energy to persevere.

Even though this happened a few years later, I am throwing this in for good measure. There was a tapping on our front door at 6:30 a.m. It certainly was not the mailman.

As I opened the door, I noticed that in our driveway was one of those tow trucks. Although I was not clearly awake, that got my attention. I inquired of the man wearing gloves and standing on my doorstep, "Can I help you?"

"Yeah," he said, "Are you Frank Rambaldo?"

I knew that was a trick question because not everyone called me by my dad's name.

"Yeah, I'm Frank," was my reply. After all, Michele was right there. She knew that I was sometimes known as Frank.

"Well," he said "National City Bank has sent me…"

I began to tell him my side of the story, a truthful one, but by the look on his face, it was one he hears many, many times a day. Remember, he does this for a living.

"You see, I have been arguing with the bank for quite sometime now about sending my car payments into Kentucky and them not being posted on time."

He was not a bit interested. Instead, he inquired if we had anything in the vehicle, a black Chevy Z24, I wished to remove!

For some reason I was not mad. I wasn't intimidated. I was cooperative. I got the keys and removed our belongings.

And as Jackie Gleason used to say, "And away we gooooooooo!" And so did our Cavalier on the back of his tow truck!

I contacted Ernie, the attorney, and after a few calls, the bank somewhat admitted that there had been a mistake. Or was it an oversight they called it? If you have ever dealt with a bank when it comes to these matters, they do not make mistakes.

Well, we got our Z back.

But, as in show biz, there's nothing like a repeat performance. Another time the bank sent a guy who was not nice, not professional or as cordial like the last one. One fine day this tough guy, also with gloves on, walks into our store and, you guessed it, he, too, was looking for a Frank Rambaldo.

Now, I am a quick learner: guys with gloves, looking for Frank— there has to be a tow truck somewhere.

But there wasn't. Still, I had my suspicions.

So, I asked him, "Who are you and whom do you represent?"

His reply, "I am looking for Frank. Is he in?"

Since I was with a customer, I shook my head, as in no.

Well, he simply turned and left. Thank God, I thought. I watched him out of the corner of my eye. He got in his small pickup truck and appeared to be leaving. All of a sudden, I see his reverse parking lights come on, and he begins to back up. Not only back up but back up behind my fine auto. Yeah, that's right, the black beauty.

He gets out of his little truck with his gloves firmly on, and, lo and behold, he has some sort of portable "hook-'em up Charlie" device!

I thought, unbelievable. They're at it again! This time, I wanted justice. I once again called The Man of Justice, Ernie, the attorney.

He couldn't believe what I was saying. Probably because I was talking so fast, he couldn't understand me. But one thing he does know is my track record. If I appear to be ranting and raving, if I am angry and excited, it's a sure bet I am telling him the truth.

As we all know by now, the truth will set you free. Ernie called the bank, and once again, they said they may have made an oversight. The car would be returned that day.

I took matters into my own hands and took the fine bank to small claims court. And true to form, they admitted there might have been some oversights. After reviewing the facts and my demands, it was ruled that the bank was at fault. They agreed to grant me two free payments, dissolved any late fees, and finally they would not send out hook 'em up Charlie unless they sent me a certified letter first.

Well, that never happened again. Moral of the story: It takes a lot of mistakes for a bank to admit they made one. But if you, the consumer, even appear to have failed in your part of the agreement, they pull the trigger. BANG! BANG!

The year 1996 was not a kind one to our family. Yet, it was a year that showed us that if you're paying attention, His Word is true. He is the only Man of His Word whom we should trust unconditionally. His words, when read and kept in your heart, will show you the way to maneuver through life's trials and tribulations. And they are the only words that give us everlasting hope.

The year 1996 showed our children and those that were paying attention that if you put your faith and focus on something other than the Almighty Buck, you can and will survive as a family. Trials are a part of each of our lives, and by knowingly picking up our cross daily and following Jesus and His Word, we, too, will somehow walk on water. It most likely will be a crossing we wouldn't choose to make, but He will carry us through. Like Moses, we will begin to develop a Red Sea scrapbook of memories of when we were in the wilderness when God pulled us out. He will find a way out of no way! God wants you to know His credentials are good.

When you pass through the waters, I will be with you; And when you pass through the rivers, they will not sweep over you. When you walk through the fire, you will not get burned; the flames will not set you ablaze. Isaiah 43: 2

1993 Dion's 55th Birthday
Michele and Chuck with their Rock n' Roll Idol

1943 Grandma Mary
and Aunt Cora

Chuck with Godparents
Charlie and Jean Presti

CHAPTER 14

MUSIC TO YOUR EARS AND SPIRIT

When others are troubled, needing our sympathy and encouragement, we can pass on to them this same help and comfort God has given us. 2 Corinthians 1: 4.

I think the one universal high is music. It comes in many forms and types, but for me it has been a natural high since I can remember. We got our indoctrination from Mom. My mom's side possessed all the musical talent. The Paschulls were gifted musicians. And to this day Mom starts her day with music. At first, it was "the beat" that got my attention. As life progressed, the spirit in the message took its place.

I have been listening to Dion's *The Best of the Gospel Years* since the mid '80s. One song that stands out is "Sweet Surrender." Michele and I recently saw Dion. We have not missed any of his Cleveland appearances since he came out of retirement in the late '80s. Although we love his Italian rock and roll, the highlight of every concert is when he "testifies" how the Lord took his cravings for drugs and alcohol when he couldn't give them up. Now, when you truly listen to the lyrics of "Sweet Surrender," every line has a real meaning, and as we grow older, a real meaning for each of us.

Sweet Surrender

Thought I was bad, and I had to get good.
Thought I was smart, but I misunderstood.
Felt I was weak, and I had to get strong
I was sure I was right then I found I was wrong.
Thought I was lost, and I had to get found.
They called me square, so I tried to get round.
Felt I was lazy, and I had to get busy.
Swore I was high, but I was just plain dizzy.

You see, but now I really know.
Like I never knew before
Lord come a knockin'
And I finally opened up the door.
No doubt about it.

Oh, Sweet Surrender
Oh, Oh Sweet Surrender
Oh Sweet Surrender
Yeah Sweet Surrender
Totally Totally
Oh Sweet Surrender
You lift me higher
Love how you lovin' me
Oh Sweet Surrender.

Oh Sweet Surrender
What can I do for you?
Felt I was bored, so I made a switch
Thought I was poor, and I had to get rich
I was sure I was crazy, and I had to get sane.
It wasn't enough so I changed my name
Thought my image needed a pat on the back
I thought my ego needed a Cadillac
Then I was sitting in the driver's seat
I was feeling low
And still incomplete
And now I really know
No doubt about it
I never knew before
Lord, come a knockin'
And I finally opened up the door

Thank You Lord!
Thank you Lord!
Oh, Sweet Surrender

Lift me Higher
Saying
Oh Sweet Surrender
Amazing is your love
Of Sweet Surrender
You make me happy
Oh Sweet Surrender
You know I finally stopped my running
Oh Sweet Surrender
Finally stopped my running
Oh Sweet Surrender
Don't have to run
no more
Know exactly who I am
Let it go
Amazing is your Love
Of Sweet Surrender
You lift me higher
Higher
Higher
You lift me Higher
No Doubt about it
Saying
Oh Sweet Surrender
Laying back in Jesus arms
Oh Sweet Surrender
Let it go Let it go
Don't work your way to Heaven
Let it go
He loves you where you are
Let it go
Let it go
(Sweet Surrender©1980 Dion DiMucci)
Reprinted with permission.

It's that simple—just surrender.

We have been fortunate enough to meet with Dion on two occasions. I even got to speak with him on WMJI Radio on the legendary DJ Norm N. Nite's show. I can tell you from my personal experience that he is the real deal. What you see is what you get: an honest-to goodness, God-loving man. When he was with Michele and me, I felt a certain spiritual connection such as I have shared with very few individuals in my journey thus far.

Dion wrote a book entitled *The Wanderer*. If you can find a copy, it's great reading. In Chapter 15 entitled Jack, he explains that it was his father-in-law, "the flesh-and-blood proof of another human being, someone who had been there and back, who could understand what had happened to me, not because he'd read about a case like mine, but because he'd been a case like mine."

For me, the mystery of God isn't found in flashy miracles and spiritual fireworks. It's in the way He uses simple, ordinary people and everyday situations to get the job done. I almost drove myself off a bridge. It was that close when God stepped in.

His father-in-law, Jack Butterfield, also knew what life was like inside a bottle. Dion says truth has a ring that reaches down right into your spirit. Jack had just lost his thirty-eight-year-old son to alcoholic convulsions. In the midst of all his pain, his father-in-law told Dion he was an alcoholic. "Pray. Get on your knees talk to Him. He's your best friend. Trust Him."

"So I tried it. I got down on my knees and I talked to God. Take it away—the booze and the pills and the dark places inside. Something happened on April 1, 1968. I said goodbye to drinking and drugs and all the devouring needs they fed forever. I was three months shy of my twenty-ninth birthday, but that night I felt like I climbed out of a womb for the very first time."

As Dion finishes his book, he illustrates the fact that I, too, believe deeply. He wants to sing about encouragement, joy and the peace that flows like a river to the sea. "I can't preach, but I can tell a story. And it seems to help when you know the story's true."

Another song of Dion's that speaks to me is "Hymn to Him." I have listened to this song nearly every day from 1986 until the present. It touches my spirit so much I think I will start any talks I give on this book with this tune. It's on Dion's *The Best of Gospel Years*.

I want to share the supernatural lyrics with you.

HYMN TO HIM

Do you walk in the shadows?
Are your dreams swept with fear?
Does your heart fill with sadness?
With the night drawing near?

Do you yearn for the moment
When you'll be safe and warm?
Do you search for the shelter
From life's oncoming storm?

(Chorus)

Come to Him through the darkness
Come to Him through the rain
Walk with Him from misfortune
Walk with Him from the pain
He's the light of salvation
He's the head never bowed
He's the first step of wisdom
He's the sun through the clouds
Walk with Him.

If the winds of disaster
Have blown hard through your night
And the dreams you have cherished

Can't begin to take flight
Take His hand through the sunlight
Lift your head high above
Let your heart flow forever
With the warmth of His love
(Repeat Chorus)
Blend your life with His blessings
Drink from the wine of tomorrow
Yesterday must be banished
With the seeds of your sorrows.

Do you walk in the shadows?
Are your dreams swept with fear?
Does your heart fill with sadness?
With the night drawing near?
Do you yearn for the moment
When you'll be safe and warm?
Do you search for the shelter
From life's oncoming storm?
(Repeat Chorus)
Words and music ©1980 Dion DiMucci and Bill Tuohy
Reprinted with permission.

We all know Elvis as The King of Rock 'n Roll, but actually he was the king of modern gospel. With all his hits, with all his sold out rock and roll concerts, with all his record- breaking performances, with being named Entertainer of the Century (eat your heart out, you Sinatra fans)—it was only for his gospel recordings that he received awards. His renditions of songs like "Amazing Grace," "Peace in the Valley," "He Touched Me," "Crying in the Chapel," "How Great Thou Art," and "Where Could I Go but to the Lord?" have touched the hearts of millions. These tunes are on a compact disc titled *Elvis Presley: Gospel Favorites*. Other songs that have touched my spirit are "Get Together" by the Youngbloods; "Spirit in the Sky" by Eric Greenbaum, and "They Don't Understand" by Sawyer Brown.

Over the past few years, contemporary Christian music has become a part of our radio dial. There are many new musicians who are spreading His Word through their music.

The words of others with whom we come in contact can also be uplifting. Please remember that back in 1985, I seemed to see no way out. But one of the most important promises God delivered on for me and my family was the unity of our family and the ability to achieve that which we chose.

In 1998 and then again in 2000, Michele and I were blessed to see both of our children, first Rochelle, then Chuckie, graduate from our alma mater, John Carroll University. To parents who have prayed and scraped to make their children's way a bit easier, this is a day that only those who have sacrificed can appreciate and understand! Praise you, Lord Jesus!

Because we know God's goodness and have seen his spirit at work in our lives, we need to be a "spirit booster" in the daily walks of others. There are those relatives and friends who go beyond the call of duty or simply say the things you need to hear. So in your walk, please remember you affect others in the way you welcome, express your words of love, or simply show by example.

When others are troubled, needing our sympathy and encouragement, we can pass on to them this same help and comfort God has given us as we are told in 2 Corinthians 1: 4.

In both my brother's and my lives, we were raised with the knock on the door or the impromptu visit to a relative. During the summer months, we stayed with our dad, who lived at his mother's (our grandmother's) house in East Cleveland. There were also two sweet ladies that lived on her street, Josephine Peters and Theresa McCally. They both made Rick and me feel welcome in their homes anytime we were there. Josephine was like a loving aunt. She had lost her husband early in life and was raising her two boys, Pete and Norman. Her brother, Joe Petrello, had lost his wife and was raising his son, Raymond, under the same roof. Theresa had four children, Donny, Marilyn, Judy, and Frankie. When we walked into Theresa's home, we were made to feel as if it was a part of our home.

Most of the summer we spent playing ball with these guys from the neighborhood. A few streets over lived our cousin, Joe Comai, so we got to be friends with a few of his buddies—Paul Stern, Tommy Rudar, Nicky Delillo, and Jimmy Depeta. Needless to say, hanging with some of these dudes filled our days.

I have memories of fishing trips in Lake View Cemetery, breaking Mr. Fry's window while playing ball in the street and running when he called the police and getting my wits scared out of me when the East Cleveland Police showed up one hot summer afternoon while I was banging my drums on the third floor. They informed me that someone had called them for my "disturbing the peace." It wasn't until I made my grandmother angry a few weeks later that she blurted out, "Who do you think called the cops on you? I did!"

Then there is a vivid memory of making a great catch of a football pass from Cousin Joe and instantly hitting the front chrome bumper of a '57 Roadmaster. It sure was the master of the road. I went down for the count. The list could go on and on.

When our father was off working and supporting his family, we were left to travel with Grandma Mary. When she fired up her rusty '58 two-tone, blue and white four-door Ford, off we would go. One day our father needed to borrow that blue beauty of his mom's. Wouldn't you know, as he was coming home from his engagement, the muffler fell off. Now, we all know for a muffler to rust and fall off, it had to have been on the vehicle for quite some time.

What do you think she told our father when he informed her of what happened? "Well, Frank, it was on the car when you took it, so you better make sure it's on the car when you return it." The end result was she expected him to purchase a muffler for her—and he did!

We used to make numerous trips all around town to save a penny while Grandma shopped at three or four or five grocery stores. She never thought about time or the price of gas.

Grandma would take us to our favorite aunt's house. Aunt Cora had five children—Karen, Carole Lynn, Jeannie, Dean, and Janet. Rick and I bonded with Karen the most since she was closest to our age. We would play baseball every day with Karen and Cousin Joe down at Forest Hills Park. We would all meet and play countless innings of baseball in the hot sun for hours without the worry of some of the types of individuals we all know are out there today. And since there were no cell phones, no one checked on us until we walked in the door. Karen, was one of the finest ball players you could witness for a girl. (Is that a sexist remark?) And let me tell you, if she didn't hold her own, we would have tossed her in an instant. After all, baseball back then was for boys, particularly if you were Italian.

The depth of love we felt as we entered Aunt Cora's house at 1586 Wood Avenue in Cleveland Heights, Ohio, was one rarely experiences in life. There were no conditions—no condemnations, no rules, just an honest, open feeling of being welcomed and loved. Our Aunt Cora is now in her mid-eighties, and she still displays the warmth she did back in the '60s. She never complains about her health problems or any family matters that may be on her mind; she is interested in you. She was one example in my life where actions always spoke louder than words. She walked the walk. She did not just talk the talk.

Our other aunt, actually great-aunt, was our grandmother's sister, Aunt Frances. She lived in an Italian neighborhood, Collinwood,

Ohio. Her husband, Uncle Jack, was a war veteran. Also, our cousin, Corrine Garnik, was famous for her unexpected uplifting visits. The feeling on that side of town was also one that was always cheery, always welcoming and not judgmental.

Then there is my Godmother Jean. Her image in my mind's eye is one of genuine love. That godly smile of hers always said, "You are mine and I am yours." Her family has owned and operated a legendary bakery business in Little Italy, Presti's Bakery. I still can't wait for an excuse to drop in and pick up "the best bread man has ever tasted." It is a meal in itself. But the true ingredient that makes both their bread rise and their love for us grow is a spiritual connection that's hard to explain unless you, too, have or have had an Aunt Cora, Aunt Frances, Josephine Peters, Theresa McCally, or Godmother Jean in your life. I surely hope you have experienced such love.

I told you of my positive experience with Sister John Vianney. There was another nun with whom I reunited on my twenty-fifth grade school reunion in 1989—Sister Peter Clayver. She was another individual with whom I felt the presence of God. She saw my sincere love and interest in my grade school, and when the reunion was over, she gave me a small pin that simply read "I Love St. Mary's." At the time, she was suffering with a physical ailment, but she never let you know it. Although Sister Peter Clayver has passed on, she is one of those individuals whose spirit lives on in my memory.

It wasn't until later in life that I began to see and appreciate the sacrifices of my other cousins, JoAnn (Paschull) Odell and Marilyn (Farinacci) Paschull. JoAnn was somewhat older and distant in my childhood years. But I have to credit her for the reason I never chose to smoke. Remember one of the givens growing up in the '50s and '60s was being "cool" and having a "pack of smokes" on you at all times. Once when I might have been nine or ten years old, I was watching JoAnn puffing on a cigarette. I told her how neat she looked "Neat? You think smoking is cool? Here, try it."

I grabbed the lighted cigarette from her hands and eagerly puffed away. I still can recall choking and choking. My senses were engulfed with a drowning feeling. Thanks to JoAnn, I've never taken another puff.

In later years, I recall JoAnn and her husband Tom driving out of our driveway in Willoughby in his fancy T-Bird and how pretty she was. Although I don't recall her being either spiritual or religious when I was young, JoAnn was probably the first born-again in our family. When she and Tom used to visit from Seattle when our children were young, she would openly share how the Lord had worked in her life, and she would pray out loud for our family.

Recently, I was talking with her and sharing family stories. I asked her how she found her way spiritually. She told me she was originally an agnostic; her instruction in the Catholic faith had turned her off. She also stated that she studied white witchcraft and the works of Edgar Cayce. She also remembered that at one point in her life, she was a little down and attended a prayer service. One Christian woman friend looked at her and told her, "Christ died for you and your sins."

She replied, "Well, who asked Him to do that?"

Both JoAnn and Tom have practiced their Christian ministry since 1970. Now when she calls, it is always music to my ears and spirit.

But our cousin Marilyn was like our older sister. She was the one who babysat us. In retrospect, she is a woman to be admired for the way she silently handled her crosses in life. What a strong, strong woman. She basically raised her two children, Gina and Johnny, on her own.

I guess I was either blind to those family members around me who also have been carrying their crosses for years and years, or I was simply too young to look around me, look away from me, stop focusing on me. I couldn't see that there was heavy, heavy wood on the shoulders of everyone I came in contact with. It was only after I focused on Him did He allow me to see this. He also taught me to share and witness my faith with others.

Even as I was writing this chapter, God intervenes and allows me to see how a bit of "seed planting" can take hold. Funny, how fast you become the older generation. I find myself wanting to pass this knowledge on to those close family members, and many times I get short or to the point. I guess that's why I spent awhile getting in touch with my emotions. It's not a guy thing, but it's a God thing! And that's what really matters.

Another thing that has been on my mind for years is why doesn't our society recognize the real value in a parent? If you, as a single parent, or you and your spouse have tried your best to raise your child or children, please give yourself a round of applause. It is my belief that we should all C.L.A.P. for parents like you: Cherish, Love, Appreciate, Parents.

Even God said in certain circumstances, you can divorce your spouse. But what would justify people divorcing their obligations to their children?

Since the passing of our son-in-law, Mat Bailey, I will do my best to try to convey the amount of pain and sorrow our families have so far endured. Someone once said that when God takes someone from you, He replaces that someone with something else. In our case, he gave us Mia! Mia was born on Mother's Day, May 8, 2005. What a heavenly experience for our families that day! Who would have known that just three weeks later her father Mat would die? Mat was only twenty-seven, yet in the time I knew him I feel he lived his life to the fullest—in reverse order, perhaps, seventy-two years. Mat was the kind of individual whose charismatic personality made him a standout. In addition, he was always the one who was there for anyone who needed his expertise. He was as handy and skillful with his hands as anyone I have ever met. I thought I was a proud papa when both of our children, Rochelle and Chuckie, were born. I took a distant backseat to how proud Mat was when he saw, held, and kissed Mia. You couldn't have witnessed a more proud and happy father. In many ways, Mat is still with us daily. His little Mia shows many of his fine traits. She is one unique gift!

There have been many long and sleepless nights since we lost Mat. As with any family that has experienced a loss, there have been many, many emotional outbursts, many, many differences of opinion. The hard lesson Michele and I are still trying to learn is—we can no longer try to make things right for our children. They are adults. We can only offer our love to both our daughter and granddaughter. Michele and I are proud and amazed by what a loving and caring single parent our daughter has become. Rochelle has become a single parent of whom we stand in awe. She has had to weather an undue amount of storms that most individuals never have to face—all at the tender age of thirty. She does it, for the most part, in her own way. Yet, she continues to search for what is best for her and her lovely daughter. We C.L.A.P. for her.

CHAPTER 15

IT'S ALL ABOUT REPENTANCE

Be on guard! If your brother sins, rebuke him; and if he repents, forgive him. And if he sins against you seven times a day, saying, "I repent," forgive him. Luke 17: 3-4.

Behold, I stand at the door and knock. Revelation 3: 20.

As for me and my house, we will serve the Lord. Joshua 24: 15.

How can a young man keep his way pure? By living according to God's word. Psalm 119: 9.

I was fortunate enough to see Reverend Billy Graham at Cleveland Municipal Stadium in the '90s. It was like watching a prophet from the Bible. When you look at him and listen to his message, you just know he is a man of his word.

One thing he said that day still stays with me: "Many of the difficulties we experience as Christians can be traced to a lack of Bible study and reading."

Wow! Please don't get me wrong. I am not saying that once you are born again, once the Holy Spirit, The Comforter, enters your life, the game is over. No problems! No worries! No stresses! No. That's not the way it is; you still remain a mere mortal.

The only difference is you are now equipped to handle the problems, worries and stresses. In my case, one day at a time. And I am not saying that you will not be haunted by past memories of bad decisions, bad family relationships or bad thoughts. It's more than twenty years later and I still fight such feelings daily. But I know how to fight such thoughts, and I know He will remind me of His promises simply by staying in His Word. He has a covenant with his sheep. *I know mine and mine know me.* John 10: 14.

I am still a walking wounded soldier for Christ. The difference between me now and me then is I that am walking forward. I may have wounds from day to day, week to week, year to year, but I don't allow them to swallow me up. I may wallow in self-pity about how life sometimes isn't fair, but then I look at The Cross and I get it. I am still a walking wounded soldier of Christ by choice—a choice I made in desperation. The human side of me still would not choose the path my life and my family had to endure since 1985. I know it is a path I could not have traveled without spiritual and divine guidance.

Remember at the outset of this book I told you I was running on empty. Or was I running from God? I had to learn that my sin of pride had blinded me to the fact that I had to repent to my Lord and Savior. But why should I? Hadn't I been working hard on being good And by being good, I was working my way into heaven. Wrong! Once I experienced the need to repent, and once I chose to, I received God's grace guaranteed by the Holy Spirit. It involves one decision to accept the Lord's death as payment for all of our sins.

Remember the Parable of the Prodigal Son (Luke 15: 11-32)? The prodigal son never stopped being a member of his father's family, but while he was off living a life of sin, he was deprived of the blessings of the relationship. As soon as he sought forgiveness, the blessings were restored.

It still is a path that is frustrating to explain and share. Yet, it is my belief that once you have been sanctified in the shed blood of Jesus Christ, you can freely share with others the frailty of your being. You can talk about your innermost dark secrets. Others will share with you things they may be fearful of admitting until they hear your story from your lips.

I believe one is truly cured when he or she can proclaim how Jesus has lifted one's human sinfulness. It may be the clinical depression you battled or battle. It may be the addiction to alcohol, pills, or drugs. Whatever it is, how you choose to handle it reveals if you are truly cured. I pray that others see the light before they, too, hit the wall. We walk by faith, not by sight, and trust the Lord.

Now if your children are adults with lives of their own, you think, you pray that some of your cross carrying was viewed by them in gold-circle seating.

By gold-circle, I mean up close and personal. Your children and family, for the most part, are sitting in the front row of your life. Sometimes they get to see a great feature film, and other times, they view a horror flick. We have to be seed planters for them also. The hard part is watching our adult children make unwise choices. It's another lesson we are learning. We come to realize they must make their own decisions and make them in God's time.

Just because I set an example or just because I think that we all should strive to live by God's code of conduct, "it ain't necessarily so." When I am laid to rest, there will be words about how a husband, a son, a dad, a papa lived by being "a man of his word." But the real message is that he fell off the mountain side. Although he was blinded by his own pride, he rose again to the mountaintop on the wings of a dove. He finally saw the light. And he did so by following the real Man of His Word—Jesus Christ.

I can't tell you how scared, I was the night of December 20, 1999. Around 3:00 a.m., our son, Chuckie, who was then twenty-two, woke us. He was terrified. Just a few hours earlier, he was calmly watching TV when Michele and I had kissed him goodnight. Now, he was in our darkened bedroom saying things like; "I'm going to die. I can't sit still." He was in a state of fear I had experienced before. But then it was I who needed help.

He also said, "I can't tell you what's wrong...you'll be mad at me." Well, Michele decided that we needed to call the doctors, Dave and Semele in Cincinnati, my brother-in-law and his wife.

Chuckie got on the phone, and after a few of their questions, he confessed. "I was smoking marijuana," he said. "I had smoked it before, but never did I have this kind of reaction." They explained to him that in time he would be all right.

After the truth was out, he seemed a bit calmer and very remorseful. I asked him where the stuff was. And he showed me. I took him to the toilet and we both flushed it down. I knew then that he was sick enough to ask for help. I asked him in our living room, in the wee hours of the morning, if he was ready to surrender his life to Jesus. He replied, "Yes!"

After that night when he woke us, Chuckie sent us this letter.

Dear Mom and Dad,

Being so busy and whatnot it was hard for me to keep sight of the most important day of my life. Looking back, it was the worst but how it altered my life made it the best.

December 20, 1999, was a day I thank God for. Looking back, if I wouldn't have had the courage to let you see me at my weakest point, God knows where I would be today. You both held my hand when I walked through hell and for that I am forever grateful. I created my own prison, and I needed both of you to help free me of my chains.

But what I am most grateful for is that a year ago you both gave me life again. I had no direction, I had no peace. The voices I heard were stronger than that of a thousand men. You both helped to silence them. Though I thought I knew Him well, it was both of you who introduced me to the Lord. And every day I thank Him for that. I let myself die only to transform spiritually. I found myself on my knees praying to a Lord I had all [but] forgotten. He was still listening.

Your son, Chuckie

Chuckie's letter reminds us that the very first word spoken publicly by Jesus was "Repent." Would you like to be forgiven for all of your sins and live with God forever?

Tony Evans, writing for Good News Publishers, suggests this prayer:

Dear Heavenly Father, I am a sinner and cannot save myself. I believe that Your Son Jesus Christ died on the cross in my place for my sins and rose from the grave to give me salvation. I now accept the Lord Jesus Christ as my personal Savior, trusting Him alone to give me eternal life and a relationship with You. Amen.

Michele's father, David Morad, Sr., was another man in my life who was a man of his word. Whenever I called on his daughter at their home in Lyndhurst, he always made me feel welcome and a part of his family. Over the years, when he called me "son" it felt real. He was, in my view, what a father, husband and man should be. Like me, he, too, was a sinner. His cowboy boots are hard to fill.

The Lord gave him the send-off from this earth that he deserved although we did not know it at the time. He went into the hospital for what was termed a minor operation. He had had open heart surgery a few years before. In the early morning before his operation, his entire family gathered around his bedside. His smile, his upbeat attitude and his confidence are what I remember about that day. In retrospect, God allowed him to see how loved he was. I know he did not think it would be the last time he would be with us, but God also gave all of us a gift that morning. He allowed us to share with David his last moments here on this earth. Many times since his passing, I will be doing a certain thing, experiencing a certain trial or listening to a fantastic drummer, and warm thoughts of past experiences with him remind me that he is there with each of us.

2005 Mia Bailey- Our Heart   2005 Rochelle and Mat

2005 Mat & Mia- Proud DAD

CHAPTER 16

CROSS CARRYING

Greater is He who is in me, than he who is in the world. 1 John 4: 4.

I can do all things through Jesus Christ who strengthens me.
Philippians 4: 13.

I have come to bring fire to the earth. Now families will be split apart. Three in favor of me and two against. Luke 12: 49-53.

I have to remind myself constantly that there is no reason for my life to be easier or more protected from evil, sickness or depression than others' just because I profess to be born again. And I often have to inform my friends and family that I am no better than others, nor do I have any magic powers that allow me to walk through fire just because, as they remind me, 'You're one of those Born-Agains!' We all experience our share of trials and tribulations. We all get depressed at times.

In *The Road Less Traveled*, M. Scott Peck, M.D. defines depression as "giving up something loved or at least something that is a part of ourselves and familiar." He further states, "The ultimate goal of life remains the spiritual growth of the individual, the solitary journey to peaks that can be climbed only alone."

As I write this, today is a celebration for me. Exactly twenty years ago, I truly was born again. I went to sleep totally hopeless. It was my Uncle Arnold's birthday, I remember. My spirit was broken, yet when I awoke on May 8, 1986, I had a new spirit and a new beginning. I was born again. There is no reason to believe that magical event was anything other than the hand of God, releasing my worldly demons. He showed me that He is present in those who choose to repent and believe. As I write these words, it reinforces within my soul that a power greater than I exists and is here for anyone who also makes the choice to surrender.

As I witness the hardships that our children now face, the old rescuer in me wants to reach out and save them from difficulties I believe I can see coming. I have had to learn, and it is a hard lesson to learn, that they, too, must face their own problems and demons. And, yes, even our own children, who have witnessed a lesson in how to overcome the world, don't get it sometimes! They must make their choices, in their time and according to God's will. Michele and I have had many, many sleepless nights, praying for God's guidance—and it comes. But sometimes it is in small doses and always in His time.

Elvis Presley was voted Entertainer of The Century. Not bad for a truck driver from Memphis. Yet, here is a story that has often been told about Elvis. On Easter Sunday 1957, after attending church for the first time in a long while, he told his pastor, Reverend Hamill, "I am the most miserable young man you have ever seen. I have more money than I can ever spend. I have thousands of fans out there, and I have a lot of people who call themselves my friends, but I am miserable."

The one thing I can tell you honestly is that Jesus does give you inner peace—when you don't have money, when you don't have thousands of fans, when you don't have a lot of friends. For when He is the King of the inner you, His peace shines through the outer you.

There is another area of life we overlook. I simply call it Track Records. We all have one. We all build one whether we realize it or not. It is a matter of what consistent path we have chosen to take in certain key matters in life, such as family, finances, trust, honesty, love, fairness, sharing and caring.

So, when you question something one of your family members, friends or loved ones is telling you or asking you, please take a moment to reflect upon that individual's track record. Our society uses such a device in almost every area the world labels as important to know.

In school, you get a report card for every grade. In operating a car, your driver's license has your history, bad or good. In insurance, there is a report on you and your family that depicts your track record, positive or negative. In business, you get reviews that decide how far and how fast up the ladder you will climb. In health, your doctors keep an active chart of your track record concerning your family history. When applying for credit, you are graded on your past track record. In court, there is a track record of how many offenses or lack of them you have committed. Even at horse races you are given a program so you can review the horses' histories and make a logical decision on how they will win, place or show.

In life, then, why is it that we seldom look at our loved ones' track record and take that into account or thank them for how long and hard they have chosen to carry their cross for us. Yet, we often seem to offer absolution to those who have fallen short!

Oh, I know we are to be good Christians and all forgiving. Or are we? Does Jesus call us to be Christianly correct? I think not.

If a brother sins against you, go to him privately and confront him with his fault. If he listens and confesses, you have won back a brother. But if not, take one or two others with you and go back again, proving everything you say by these witnesses. If he refuses to listen, then take your case to the church, and if the church verdict favors you, but he won't accept it, then the church should excommunicate him. *And I tell you this: whatever you bind on earth is bound in heaven.* Matthew 18: 15-18.

He calls us to read His Word, learn from it and see if we and those within our life's circle live up to or align with it. If not, we are to offer His teaching. But if others choose, no matter who they may be, family included (no free passes here), to walk their own walk, I believe that is when we analyze their track records. If this is just a bump in the road of life, we keep praying that God may intervene and open their eyes.

If their actions are or have been very consistent, trust them, believe in them. We normally don't stray far from our path of life. And normally it is a path we have chosen or been guided to. If you have chosen Christ, He has the best track record you will ever receive. For He told us, *I will never leave you nor forsake you.* Hebrews 13: 5-6. And in Romans 8: 35, 37-39 Paul informs us, *Who can separate us from the love of Christ? Can affliction or anguish or persecution or famine, or nakedness, or danger or sword? No, in all these things we are more than victorious through Him who loved us, For I am persuaded that neither death nor life, Nor angels nor rulers, Nor things present, nor things to come, nor powers, nor height, nor depth, nor any other created thing will have the power to separate us from the love of God that is in Christ Jesus our Lord.*

I have already expressed what Jesus instructs us to do, but in case it has not sunk in, please remember His words, *Take up thy cross and follow me daily.* Luke 9: 23.

In my journey, there have been countless days of bearing the burden of that cross. But He has always helped me in shouldering my struggles and always keeps His word.

I am about to share another instance of what I feel was true repentance witnessed. It has been my sad experience to say that God does not always give us the resolutions with our family, loved ones or acquaintances we seek, cherish or think are "right". But I can tell you that God does work in strange and mysterious ways. I believe that one of my crosses, after I knew what true repentance was, was to find any form of it in others.

It was not until the tragic loss of our son-in-law, Mathew Bailey, that I witnessed one of His purposes for my dark time of 1985.

One morning while showering, God put on my heart that I should try to reach out to the individual, Jeffrey Simmons, who was operating the golf cart that Mat and others had been goofing around on the night Mat lost his life. I thought about it, reflected upon it and prayed about it for some time.

My mind's memory saw the most sorrowful individual of the thousands who passed before Mat's casket in June of 2005. It was Jeffrey Simmons. I was reminded of that December day in court at the sentencing of Jeffrey Simmons.

I have never witnessed a more remorseful individual in my life. And, believe me, my soul has been seeking it for years. Now, He was telling me that this was a part of my mission He had been preparing me for since 1985—to reach out to one whose actions most people would question.

Well, I had to learn that our walk with Him is for His purpose, not what we feel our purpose should be. So, I chose to take the necessary steps to see if I could visit Jeffrey Simmons in jail.

Since I was neither family nor a personal friend, I had to seek Jeffrey's permission to see him. It took three trips from our home in North Royalton before I could finally talk with him. My third experience with Jeff was that of an individual who had true remorse for his actions.

I was also inspired to bring Jeffrey a Bible with his name embossed on it. I had highlighted the Scripture verses that allowed me to make it through one day, one hour, one minute. I thank God for allowing me to witness "the planting of a seed."

CALVARY

Whose side are you on?
Jesus Christ- Lord and Savior,
Openly Repentant Sinner,
or the Openly Defiant Sinner.

CHAPTER 17

THE CHOICE: **IN** OR **OF** THIS WORLD

The Holy Spirit soon came to comfort them and empower them to spread the gospel of Salvation. Acts 2: 1-4.

A true Christian, living an obedient life, is a constant rebuke to those who accept the moral standards of this world. Billy Graham

The world would love you if you belonged to it; for I chose you to come out of the world, and so it hates you. John 15: 19.

When you accept Jesus Christ as your personal Savior, and you surrender your life to Him, the answer becomes clear and the choices, though they may be difficult, are easier. You focus on that which is above, and not below. You walk in this world and cease to become a part of it.

I began to learn these truths in 1985. I realize I had three choices then:

STAY IN 1985 – Harbor my wounds and replay those horrors over and over again for the rest of my life.

DIE IN 1985 – Give into those "deep, dark death" thoughts and end it all.

SURRENDER IN 1985 – Become born again in Spirit and surrender my will to God.

Thanks to God and a lot of spiritual friends I chose the last one. But, believe me, it was a choice. As in my case, when I asked Jesus to come into my life, the truth was I could no longer control or handle the situations I was facing. There was no way out. There were no bolts of lightning from the sky, earth-shattering displays or instant miraculous cures. It was a long, drawn-out evolution.

As Dion DiMucci tells in his book, *The Wanderer*, he was an alcoholic and drug addict, but when, in 1968, he asked Christ into his life, the desire and craving for both alcohol and drugs were gone in an instant. That's what I expected in my case. That's not what occurred.

As I approached the end of writing this book, concerned parties would ask, "Chuck, is the book finished?"

I would always reply, "Soon. Real soon."

I remember some wisecracker saying, "Come on, already. I can help you finish. Just write two words—The End."

Of course, that got me thinking about another movie, strangely called *The End*. As a man who learns he does not have long to live, Burt Reynolds seeks answers as to Why me? He spots a secluded lake and decides to end it. He jumps in, clothes and all, and swims a great length off shore. When he reaches a point where he feels comfortable, he looks up to the sky and proclaims, "Here I come, Lord." He takes a final breath and submerges himself. While underwater, he hears his daughter's voice say, "Why did Daddy do it?" He reconsiders his choice and struggles to push himself above the water's surface. Exhausted and gasping for air, he shouts, "I wanna live. I wanna live."

It is at this point he appears to surrender and starts making deals with God. "Help me, Lord, and I promise I won't try this again. I'll be a better father, a better man. I promise to obey every one of the Ten Commandments. Save me and I'll give you fifty percent of everything I make. I'm talking gross, Lord."

As he gets close to shore and safety, he begins to realize that he's going to live, and he begins to renegotiate with God. "I'll give you ten percent of everything I make."

During the past twenty-plus years, I, too, have found myself trying to renegotiate with God. I struggled with just how much I would "witness and share" in this book. As my father used to say, "Don't pull any punches, son." And that's what my heavenly Father has asked with the surrendering of my will.

Jesus' calling of me was not once. It was not twice. It was not one day. It was not one year. It was over a long period of time. He had been calling me for a long, long while, but I had not listened to His call.

I now know He wanted to make sure He got my full attention. He took almost one full year of me being in hell to answer my plea. It has taken more than twenty years just to begin to grow in my knowledge of His love and what He can do. At John Carroll we were taught that ninety percent of everything we seek to do is preparation and the remaining ten percent is execution. As Peter Drucker, the father of management, wrote, "Plans are only good intentions unless they immediately degenerate into hard work." So it goes with our faith. Sooner or later, God places us all in certain situations where we can talk about our good intentions all we like, but such talk has to degenerate into witnessing and the planting of seeds.

When I was going through my deep waters in 1985 and 1986, and when I first "got it," I thought it was time to tell my story, His story. It's amazing that when you "get it," you are very anxious to share it. I had to learn another lesson. It's in God's time, not our time. It is now apparent to me that for the past twenty-plus years, He was preparing me to execute the "planting of His seeds." And like Jerry and Grace Wrobel and other members of the prayer group, I had to learn that not only is it difficult sharing your experience, but it's also difficult watching those not listening and not "getting it." Many are called but few are chosen.

Recently, my attorney, Ernie Sobieski, invited me to a Men's Catholic Renewal. Well, because it was Ernie, I went. At first, there was nothing exciting about the event. Then the headliner, Father Larry Richards, a Catholic priest from Erie, Pennsylvania, was introduced.

The first words out of his mouth were "How many of you were raised Catholic and attended Catholic schooling?"

A majority of the hands, including mine, went up.

His second question was "How many of you think you're going to heaven because of your good works?"

Once again, a majority of hands waved in the air.

"Wrong!" he shouted out. "How many of you think you're going to heaven because you've been a good person?"

Once again, the majority in attendance lifted their hands up.

"WRONG!" he bellowed. "Do you know what Jesus will say to you if that's your answer? 'Go to Hell!'"

That got my attention!

Then he followed with "Hold up your Bibles."

When there was just air hanging in the air, he exclaimed, "Just what I thought. You'd better get one if you don't have one already. There's no dirt piled over you yet. You still have time to learn. You still have time to change."

I realize what Father Larry was trying to emphasize to us men, the spiritual leaders of our families. It was simple: Maybe we were not trained properly in spite of our Catholic upbringing and schooling.

Scripture has all you need to understand the "facts of life" at any age.

The Bible

His Word

Get one.

Read one.

Pass it on!

One of the main purposes for this book is to explain how I realized the above facts Father Larry was trying to explain to us old timers. It was a little late in life but, nonetheless, a lesson well learned.

If you wish to learn more about Father Larry and his ministry, please visit his website at www.reasonforourhope.com or pay him a visit at St. Joseph's Parish, Bread of Life Community, 147 West 24th Street in Erie, Pennsylvania 16502
1-814-452-2982

In his book, *The Reason for My Hope*, Charles Stanley states, "*If I were to look to the headlines of the newspaper or hear the opening lines of virtually any newscast....If I were to look only at the scores of people I know who struggle daily with severe problems—diseases that have been diagnosed as terminal, marriages that are crumbling, children who are rebellious, communities that are being shattered by racism or eaten away by poverty, homes that are being destroyed by alcohol or chemical addictions...If I were to listen to only people who are seeking to escape the horrors of present-day abuse or coping with the fear-evoking memories of past abuse...it would be easy to lose hope. But that is not where I look or focus my attention. I have hope today. It is unshakable hope. It is hope based upon something eternal and all-powerful. It is hope founded on good evidence. The primary reason I'm hopeful today is that I know I have a personal relationship with God through His Son, Jesus Christ. My relationship with Jesus Christ gives me an open door to everything that God has promised to His people in His Word.*"

We don't know how much time on this earth any of us has. But we do have time to choose and choices to make. If you do not already know it, choose to learn His Word. It can change your life. It did mine. I know the words that encompass most of this book are not mine. I know that there was a purpose for 1985. His purpose.

As we read in the book of Job, mankind simply does not have enough knowledge to explain why things happen the way they do. It is possible to rise above our limitations by faith in God, however, because God does know why everything happens and will work for those who love Him.

I started this book telling you how God took away my livelihood, my family, even my mind. But in His time, he restored all that and more. He gave me His inner peace that I was constantly seeking but could not find. During these past two-plus decades, I have read countless self-help books, purchased self-help tapes and compact discs and listened to many motivational speakers. All proclaimed to have "The Answer."

Along my journey, I have come to understand that there is only one book—The Bible—that truly has all the answers. And there is only one individual who speaks the Truth—Jesus Christ, our Lord and Savior.

Look at the cover of this book again. In all of our lives, Jesus asks us to make a choice. Which side of His cross will you choose? Will you choose to be IN or OF this world? In addition, please remember that our sin debt was paid in full on Calvary. The world wants us to latch on to what is selling—brand names such as Nike, Tommy Hilfiger, Mercedes, and Cadillac. In reality, there is only one name you can reply upon—Jesus! His name is truly the only brand name.

Acts 20: 24 informs us *I consider my life worth nothing to me, if only I may finish the race and complete the task the Lord Jesus has given to me, the task of testifying to the gospel of God's grace.*

So when others are troubled, needing our sympathy and encouragement, we can pass on to them this same help and comfort that God has given to us. 2 Corinthians 1:7.

My prayer is that we may learn the profound truth that when we have nothing left but God, God is enough. When Jesus is all we have, we realize he is all we need. Timothy 4: 16-17 states *Everyone deserted me...But the Lord stood at my side and gave me strength.*

He truly is the only MAN OF HIS WORD!

APPENDIX

HELPFUL BIBLE VERSES

I have found that my relationship with God through Jesus needs my choosing to read, repeat, and remain in God's word. Scripture speaks confidently. God loves us deeply, and He will meet all our needs. At times we all have emotional needs, and God's Word brings calm.

Listed below are some of the most helpful Bible verses that have aided me over the years. They have been divided into categories to aid the reader.

SALVATION/ BORN AGAIN

For what does it profit a man if he gains the whole world, and forfeits his soul? Mark 8: 36.

Truly, truly, I say unto you, unless one is born again, he cannot see the kingdom of God. John 3: 3.

Therefore, if anyone is in Christ, he is a new creation, old things have passed away; behold, new things have come.
2 Corinthians 5: 17.

He saved us, not on the basis of deeds which we have done in righteousness, but according to His mercy, by the washing of regeneration and renewing by the Holy Spirit, whom He poured out upon us richly through Jesus Christ our Savior, so that being justified by His grace we would be made heirs according to the hope of eternal life. Titus 3: 5-7.

The thief comes only to steal and kill and destroy; I came that they may have life, have it abundantly. John 10: 10.

Your sin debt is paid in full. Therefore when Jesus had received the sour wine, He said, "It is finished." And He bowed His head and gave up His spirit. John 19: 30.

And He was saying to them all, if any man come after Me, he must deny himself, and take up his cross daily, and follow me. Luke 9: 23.

Jesus said to him, "I am the way, and the truth, and the life; no one comes to the Father except through Me. John 14: 6.

If you confess with your mouth that Jesus is Lord, and believe in your heart that God raised him from the dead, you will be saved. Romans 10: 9.

Then they asked him, "What must we do to do the works God requires?" Jesus answered, "The work of God is this: to believe in the one He has sent." John 6: 28-29.

REPENTANCE/ FORGIVENESS

One of the criminals who was hanged there was hurling abuse at Him, saying, "Are you not the Christ? Save yourself and us." But the other answered and rebuking him said, "Do you not even fear God, since you are under the same condemnation? And we are indeed suffering justly, for we are receiving what we deserve from our deeds: but this man has done nothing wrong." And he was saying, "Jesus, remember me when You come into Your kingdom. And Jesus said to him, 'Truly I say to you, today you shall be with Me in paradise. Luke 23: 39-43.

"Be on guard! If your brother sins, rebuke him; and if he repents forgive him. And if he sins against you seven times a day, and returns to you seven times saying, "I repent, forgive him."
Luke 17: 3.

Jesus was saying, "Father, forgive them, for they do not know not what they are doing." Luke 23: 34.

I tell you in the same way, there will be more joy in heaven over one sinner who repents than over ninety-nine righteous persons who need no repentance. Luke 15: 7.

If a brother sins against you, go to him privately and confront him with his fault. If he listens and confesses it, you have won back a brother. But if not, then take one or two others with you and go back again, proving everything that you say by these witnesses. If he refuses to listen, then take your case to the church, and if church verdict favors you, but he won't accept it, then the church should excommunicate him. "Truly I say to you, whatever you bind on earth shall have been bound in heaven; and whatever you loose on earth shall have been loosed in heaven. Matthew 18: 15-18.

For all have sinned and fall short of the glory of God.
Romans 3:23.

When I kept silent about my sin, my body wasted away
Through my groaning all day long.
For day and night Your hand was heavy upon me;
My vitality was drained away as with the fever heat of summer.
I acknowledged my sin to You,
And my in iniquity I did not hide;
I said, "I will confess my transgressions to the Lord";
And He forgave the guilt of my sin.
Therefore, let everyone who is Godly pray to You in a time when You may be found;
Surely in a flood of great waters they will not reach him.
You are my hiding place; You preserve me from trouble;
You surround me with songs of deliverance. Psalms 32: 3-7.

And then He told them, you are to go into the world and preach the good news to everyone everywhere. Those who believe and are baptized will be saved. Those who refuse to believe will be condemned. Mark 16: 15.

THE HOLY SPIRIT

It happened that while Apollos was at Corinth, Paul passed through the upper country and came to Ephesus, and found some disciples. He said to them, "Did you receive the Holy Spirit when you believed?" And they said to him, "No, we have not even heard whether there is a Holy Spirit. And he said, "Into what then were you baptized?" And they said, "Into John's baptism." Paul said, "John baptized with the baptism of repentance, telling the people to believe in Him that was coming after him, that is, Jesus." When they heard this, they were baptized in the name of the Lord Jesus. And when Paul had laid his hands upon them, the Holy Spirit came upon them, and they began speaking with tongues and prophesying.
Acts 19: 1-6

Now God has revealed them to us by Spirit, for the Spirit searches everything, even the deep things of God. For who among men know the deep concerns of a man, except the Spirit of God? Now we have not received the Spirit of the world, but the Spirit who is from God. We also speak these things taught not by human wisdom, but in those taught by the Spirit, explaining spiritual things to spiritual people. But the natural man does not welcome what comes from God's Spirit. The spiritual person, however, can evaluate everything, yet he cannot be evaluated by anyone. For who knows the Lord's mind, that He may instruct him? But we have the mind of Christ.
1 Corinthians 2: 10-16.

For God does not give us a spirit of fear, but a spirit of power, love, and a strong mind. 2 Timothy 1: 7.

The Holy Spirit soon came to comfort them and empower them to spread the gospel of salvation. Acts 1: 9.

But when the Holy Spirit comes upon you, you will receive the power to testify about me with great effect, to the people of Jerusalem, and to the ends of the earth. Acts 1: 8.

FAMILY

Do you suppose that I have come to grant peace on earth? I tell you no, but rather division; from now on five members in one household will be divided, three against two and two against three. They will be divided, father against son, and son against father, mother against daughter and daughter against mother, mother-in-law against daughter-in-law and daughter-in-law against mother-in-law.
Luke 12: 51-53.

Don't imagine that I have come to bring peace to the earth; I did not come to bring peace, but a sword. For I came to set a man against his father, and a daughter against her mother and a daughter-in-law against her mother-in-law; and a man's enemies will be the members of his household. Matthew 10: 34-36.

Do not be bound together with unbelievers; for what partnership have righteousness and lawlessness, or what fellowship has light with darkness? Or what harmony has Christ with Belial, or what has a believer in common with an unbeliever? 2 Corinthians 6: 14-15.

DUST YOUR FEET

And whoever shall not receive you, nor hear your words, as you go out of that house or that city, shake the dust off of your feet. Matthew 10: 14.

IN OR **OF** THE WORLD

If you were of the world, the world would love its own; but because you are not of the world, but I chose you out of the world, because of this the world hates you. John 15: 19.

Behold, I send you out as sheep in the midst of wolves; so be shrewd as serpents and innocent as doves. Matthew 11: 16.

And do not be conformed to this world, but be transformed by the renewing of your mind, so that you may prove what the will of God is, that which is good and acceptable and perfect. Romans 12: 2.

Brother will betray brother to death, and father his child, and children will rise up against their parents and cause them to be put to death. You will be hated because of my name, but it is the one who has endured that will be saved. Matthew 11: 21-22.

DEPRESSION/ SUFFERING

He reveals mysteries from the darkness, and brings the darkness into light. Job 12: 22.

Behold, do not be surprised at the fiery ordeal among you, which comes upon you for your testing, as though some strange thing was happening to you; but to the degree that you share the sufferings of Christ, keep on rejoicing, so that also at the revelation of His glory you may rejoice with exultation. 1 Peter 4: 12-13.

And He said to me, "My grace is sufficient for you, for power is perfected in weakness." Most gladly, therefore, I will rather boast about my weakness, so that the power of Christ may dwell in me. Therefore, I am well content with weaknesses, with insults and distresses, with persecutions, and difficulties, for Christ's sake; for when I am weak, then I am strong.
2 Corinthians 12: 9-10.

Where there is no vision, the people perish. Proverbs 29: 18.

Be still and know that I am God. Psalm 46: 10.

Always give thanks for all things in the name of our Lord Jesus Christ, even the Father. Ephesians 5: 20.

COMFORT/ STRENGTH

My people are destroyed for lack of knowledge. Because you have rejected knowledge, I also will reject you from being my priest. Since you have forgotten the law of your God, I will also forget your children. Hosea 4: 6.

No man will be able to stand before you all the days of your life. Just as I have been with Moses, I will be with you; I will not fail you or forsake you. Joshua 1: 5.

For where your treasure is, there your heart will also be. Luke 12: 34.

And do not be conformed to this world, but be transformed by the renewing of your mind, so that you may prove what the will of God is, that which is good and acceptable and perfect. Romans 12: 2.

The word of God was written for our instruction to teach old and to train us, written on the pages of the Bible are truths of life, health, and peace. If we fall, we can stand again. Through embracing these truths, we are healed if sickness comes. As we mature our inner man through prayer and the Word, we don't have to fall prey to deception. We can effectively stand, prevail, and conquer when an attack comes. Romans 15: 4.

But this one thing I do, forgetting those things which are behind, and reaching forth unto those things which are before. Philippians 3: 13.

She continued doing this for many days. But Paul was greatly annoyed, and turned and said to the spirit, "I command you in the name of Jesus Christ to come out of her!" And it came out of her at that very moment. Acts 16: 1.

For I, on my part, though absent in body but present in spirit, have already judged him who has so committed this, as though I were present. 1 Corinthians 5: 3.

My grace is sufficient. He will call upon Me, and I will answer him; I will be with him in trouble; I will rescue him and honor him. Psalm 91: 15.

They that wait upon the Lord shall renew their strength. They shall fly like eagles. Isaiah 40: 31.

You will be bold as lions. Proverbs 28: 1.

I can do all things through Jesus Christ who strengthens me. Philippians 4: 13.

Greater is He who is in me, than he who is in the world. 1 John 4: 4.

An excellent wife who can find? For her worth is far above jewels. Proverbs 31: 10.

THE TONGUE

Death and life are in the power of the tongue and those who love it will eat its fruit. Proverbs 18: 21.

A gentle answer turns away wrath, but a harsh word stirs up anger Proverbs 15: 1.

A soothing tongue is a tree of life, but perversion in it crushes the spirit. Proverbs 15: 4.

The tongue is a small thing, but what enormous damage it can do. James 3: 5.

ENCOURAGEMENT

He shall give you the desires of your heart. Psalm 37: 4.

A good name is desired more than great wealth. Proverbs 22: 1

The righteous cry out, and the Lord hears them, and delivers them out of their troubles. Psalm 34: 17.

Cast all your cares on Me. 1 Peter 5: 7.

When you pass through the waters, I will be with you; and when you pass through the rivers, they will not sweep over you. When you walk through the fire, you will not get burned; the flames will not set you ablaze. Isaiah 43: 2.

I will never leave you or forsake you. Hebrews 13:5-6.

He reached down from heaven and drew me out of great trials. He rescued me from deep waters. Psalms 18: 16.

When others are troubled needing encouragement, we can pass on to them the same help and comfort that God has given us.
2 Corinthians 1: 7.

The wicked flee when no man pursueth: but the righteous are as bold as lions. Proverbs 28: 1.

He shall give His angels charge over thee to keep thee in all thy ways. Psalm 91: 11.

Anxiety in a man's heart weighs it down. But a good word makes it glad. Proverbs 12: 25.

For in the day of trouble He will conceal me in His tabernacle;
In the secret place of His tent He will hide me;
He will lift me up on a rock.
And now my head will be lifted up above my enemies around me,
And I will offer in His tent sacrifices with shouts of joy;
I will sing, yes, I will sing praises to the Lord. Psalm 27: 5-6.

PRIDE

Pride goes before destruction, and a haughty spirit before stumbling. Proverbs 16: 18.

We have all fallen short of the glory of God. Romans 5: 12-19.

Pride only breeds quarrels, but wisdom is found in those who take advice. Proverbs 13: 10.

FEAR

Not by might nor by power, but by my Spirit, says the Lord of hosts. Zechariah 4: 6.

Behold the fear of the Lord, that is wisdom and to depart from evil is understanding. Job 28: 28.

The Lord is my helper; I will not be afraid. What can man do to me? Hebrews 13: 6.

Do not be afraid of any man, for judgment belongs to God. Deuteronomy 1: 17.

Bible reference: *New American Standard Bible*

© 1960,1962,1963,1968,1971,1973,1975,1977,1995.

The Lockman Foundation.

HE WAS A WORKAHOLIC WHO LOST ALMOST EVERYTHING

by Chuck Rambaldo

I am an obsessive-compulsive person (aka Type A personality). In other words, I'm a perfectionist and a workaholic.

I wanted so much for my parents to get along. I acted as the peacemaker in the family, trying to make them laugh, etc. Still, they divorced in 1960 when I was ten years old. Both of them were hardworking individuals with strong moral and ethical traditions. They liked to bring my older brother and me up with standards like "Your word should mean a lot" and "Actions speak louder than words."

Until age thirty-five, I was a people pleaser, which made me very successful. I became a vice president of human resources/labor relations. Then I went through a severe depression during which I resigned from my job, lost most of the material goods we had worked so hard for and almost lost my mind. I tried almost everything for over a year. Nothing worked. Then a friend told me to try an Emotions Anonymous meeting. It probably saved my life. That was the first place I got help from others trying to survive day to day. It was so refreshing to share life experiences weekly with real people. Yet the main thing that brought me back each week was that the program was based on a Higher Power.

Spirituality has been 99.9 percent of my recovery. I had always operated as a two-dimensional being, mind and body. Then I realized I could never get myself out of the situation I was in. It was impossible. But with God, everything is possible. As I began to get into the Bible, the spirit within me began to grow. I found I was not of the world, but in it.

Over a period of time, I gradually broke the old tapes of being abandoned by my parents through reading the Word, something that was not stressed in church, even though I went every Sunday and was an altar boy for over twelve years.

The tools that helped me in my recovery are:

A weekly prayer group in Twinsburg, Ohio

Individual therapy for one and one-half years

Bible study

Reading, reading, reading books on self help

Since 1985 I have been trying not to rescue those I love (my family and co-workers).

Jesus died upon the Cross to obtain salvation for us; He is to be their Savior! Instead of trying to act like the White Knight, I try to put Jesus into my conversation with anyone who faces a crisis or appears to be without hope.

It has been more than six years since I began my walk with the Lord. Each day I try to grow my spiritual side through prayer, Christian radio or television, Scripture reading, or self-help books. My recovery has opened my eyes for the need to improve my personal relationship with God. It is hard not to try to make things happen when you have a business education background. So I begin each day with a prayer and a reminder that I do not control what will occur during that day. The first five minutes of each day I either read Scripture or a daily devotional, pray The Lord's Prayer, and review the Twelve Steps of Emotions Anonymous. It has made these past six years a true blessing!

ACCURATE DIE CASTING'S IMPROVEMENT THROUGH INVOLVEMENT

Sets Labor-Management Sights on Common Goals- *December 1979*

Excerpts taken from cover story

There are too-many problems facing any manufacturing company today.

- Accurate Die Casting is one of the larger die casters in the country.
- It is one of the few that is capable of producing in aluminum, magnesium, brass, and molded plastics.
- Back in 1974, when George Slyman acquired the company, there were:
- An adversary union/ management relationship
- Militant labor force
- Authoritarian management,
- Excessive grievances,
- Low labor effectiveness
- An uncertain economic future
- *Slyman made a quick, positive move to turn this negative situation around*
- *He placed emphasis on people*
- Utilizing the services of then-personnel manager Chuck Rambaldo, now Vice-President Human Resources/ Labor Relations.
- Rambaldo spent much of his time day-to-day in the plant (and still does) contacting the employees, getting to know each one by his or her first name. He would talk with them and was receptive to their problems.
- Contributing heavily to the excellent results achieved by Improvement Through Involvement system have been union/ management meeting held every two weeks.

- By listening to union people, by making them a part of the team, by involving them as partners in achieving company growth, even the most militant are now positive forces.
- *Accurate Die Casting is well on its way towards its objective of developing each of its employees within the concept of Every Employee a Manager.*
- Documented results cannot but point to a highly successful five-year effort:
- Product Volume, *up 37 percent*
- Direct labor employees, down 20 percent through attrition/ Supervisors, down 26 to 18
- Strikes; *none since 1975*
- Grievances; *from 45 per year down to 5 per year*
- Absenteeism; *from 8 percent down to 3.2 percent*
- Product returns; *from 4.5 percent down to 1.5 percent.*

- **A five-year success story mainly because of Owner Slyman's emphasis on people. This system represents a belief in the capabilities of the** *employees* **and how they have become committed to, and involved in, Accurate Die Casting.**

DiMucci, Dion, Davin Seay. *The Wanderer*. Beech Tree Books, October 1988.
"Sweet Surrender"
"Hymn to Him"

Emotions Anonymous. The Twelve Steps of Emotions Anonymous. Reprinted for adaptation with permission of Alcoholics Anonymous. World Services, Inc., 1939, 1955, 1976.

Evans, Tony. *Our God is Awesome*. Good News Publishers. Wheaton, IL, 1997.

Fowler, Richard A. *The Path to Serenity*. Thomas Nelson Publishers, 1991.

Graham, Billy. *The Holy Spirit: Activating God's Power in Your Life*. Thomas Nelson, 2000.

Liardon, Roberts. *How to Survive an Attack*. Albury Publishing, 1995.

MacArthur, John. "The Quest for Unity." From audiocassette series, *A Plea for Unity*, 2008.

Peck, M. Scott. *The Road Less Traveled*. Simon & Schuster, 25th anniversary edition, 2002.

Russert, Tim. *Big Russ and Me*. Random House, 2004.

Yancey, Philip. *What's So Amazing About Grace?* Zondervan, 2002.

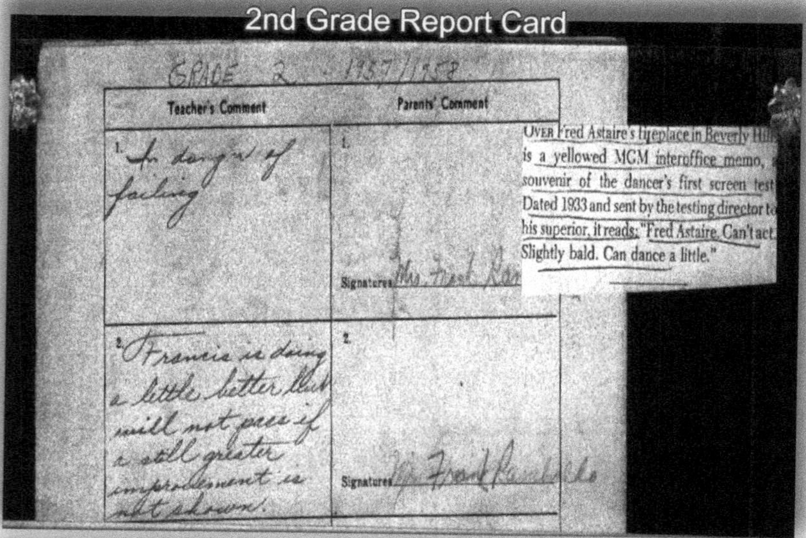
2nd Grade Report Card

Grade 2 1957/1958

Teacher's Comment	Parents' Comment
1. In danger of failing	1. Signature Mrs. Frank Ram
2. Francis is doing a little better but will not pass if a still greater improvement is not shown.	2. Signature Mrs. Frank Rambaldo

OVER Fred Astaire's fireplace in Beverly Hills is a yellowed MGM interoffice memo, a souvenir of the dancer's first screen test. Dated 1933 and sent by the testing director to his superior, it reads: "Fred Astaire. Can't act. Slightly bald. Can dance a little."

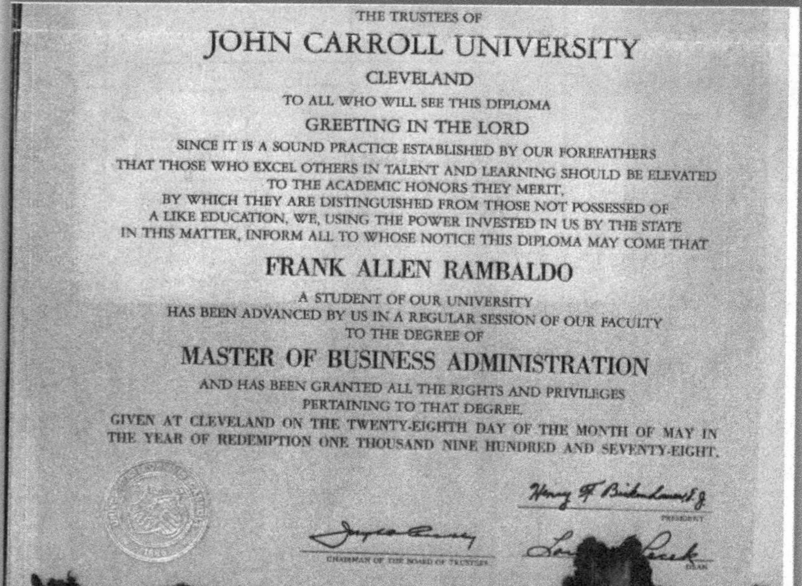

THE TRUSTEES OF

JOHN CARROLL UNIVERSITY

CLEVELAND

TO ALL WHO WILL SEE THIS DIPLOMA

GREETING IN THE LORD

SINCE IT IS A SOUND PRACTICE ESTABLISHED BY OUR FOREFATHERS THAT THOSE WHO EXCEL OTHERS IN TALENT AND LEARNING SHOULD BE ELEVATED TO THE ACADEMIC HONORS THEY MERIT, BY WHICH THEY ARE DISTINGUISHED FROM THOSE NOT POSSESSED OF A LIKE EDUCATION, WE, USING THE POWER INVESTED IN US BY THE STATE IN THIS MATTER, INFORM ALL TO WHOSE NOTICE THIS DIPLOMA MAY COME THAT

FRANK ALLEN RAMBALDO

A STUDENT OF OUR UNIVERSITY HAS BEEN ADVANCED BY US IN A REGULAR SESSION OF OUR FACULTY TO THE DEGREE OF

MASTER OF BUSINESS ADMINISTRATION

AND HAS BEEN GRANTED ALL THE RIGHTS AND PRIVILEGES PERTAINING TO THAT DEGREE.

GIVEN AT CLEVELAND ON THE TWENTY-EIGHTH DAY OF THE MONTH OF MAY IN THE YEAR OF REDEMPTION ONE THOUSAND NINE HUNDRED AND SEVENTY-EIGHT.

PRESIDENT

CHAIRMAN OF THE BOARD OF TRUSTEES

DEAN

DEPARTMENT OF THE ARMY
U. S. ARMY TRANSPORTATION SCHOOL
FORT EUSTIS, VIRGINIA 23604

ATSTC-GN

SUBJECT: Commendation

15 NOV 1972

2LT Frank A. Rambaldo, 273-48-1574
Transportation Officer Basic Course, #5-73
United States Army Transportation School
Fort Eustis, Virginia 23604

1. It is a pleasure and a privilege to commend you for attaining the
highest score in your class on the Physical Combat Proficiency Test.
Your performance is indicative of a high state of physical fitness
and a keen awareness of one of the most important responsibilities of
an officer.

2. I trust you will maintain the same high standards in all future
aspects of your career and will enjoy the success which results from
such dedication. Congratulations on this singular achievement.

3. A copy of this letter will be placed in your military personnel
records.

. T. SPRAGUE JR.
Lieut Colonel, Transportation Corps
Director, Department of Military Arts

PART B - PHYSICAL COMBAT PROFICIENCY TEST PERFORMANCE REPORT											
FIRST NAME (LAST, FIRST, MIDDLE INITIAL) RAMBALDO, FRANK A.		SERVICE NUMBER 273481574			RANK	AGE	HEIGHT	WEIGHT			
TEST NUMBER		FIRST TEST	SECOND TEST		THIRD TEST		FOURTH TEST				
DATE OF TEST											
WEATHER CONDITION		TEMP	TEMP		TEMP		TEMP				
UNIT											
EVENT	STANDARD	RAW	POINTS	RAW	POINTS	RAW	POINTS	RAW	POINTS		
40-YARD LOW CRAWL	54 SECONDS	21	160								
HORIZONTAL LADDER	50 RUNGS	77	100								
DODGE, RUN AND JUMP	24.5 SECONDS	21	100								
GRENADE THROW	15	25	80								
ONE MILE RUN	3 MINUTES AND 30 SECONDS	6:28	91								
TOTAL SCORE	471		TOTAL SCORE		TOTAL SCORE						
SCORER		SCORER		SCORER							

DA Form 705 1 Nov 68   PREVIOUS EDITIONS OF THIS FORM ARE OBSOLETE.

PHYSICAL FITNESS TESTING RECORD

RB&W

NOTICE

October 28, 1985

I am pleased to announce that Chuck Rambaldo has joined the Company as Corporate Director-Industrial Relations effective today. In this new corporate position, Chuck will be reporting directly to me.

Chuck will be responsible for supporting labor relations functions at the plants, including grievances, arbitration and contract negotiations, as well as Safety and Worker's Compensation.

Chuck has a Masters in Business Administration from John Carroll University and joins us from the Accurate Die Casting Company where he held various Industrial Relations positions over a ten-year period. His latest position with the Company was Vice President-Director of Human Resources/Labor Relations.

Please join me in welcoming Chuck to RB&W. I know he can count on your assistance and cooperation in this new position.

Kent M. Holcomb
Vice President-Human Resources

KMH:smy

Rochelle, Chuckie,
Lisa, and Ricky

Yo Chuck & Michell
Much Love

Me in "The Purple" SSR
(Super Sport Roadster)

2007
Christmas Benefit

Roro and Chuckie
at John Carroll University

1982 at home in Twinsburg
Michele with her new Charger
and of course, The KU-JEANS

The Morad's- David Sr.,
Alice, Michele,
David Jr., and Ricky

Rochelle and Chuckie with their
Ghidu (Grandfather) at his
restaurant Dave's Place

Michele and I
lanced four nights
a week in college

Dunkin Donuts David John & Alexis (our nephew & niece)

Lightning Source UK Ltd.
Milton Keynes UK
UKHW010835011022
409721UK00001B/296